What Color is Your Piggy Bank?

Entrepreneurial Ideas for Self-Starting Kids

written by Adelia Cellini Linecker

Lobster Press ™

To my son, Michael.
– *Adelia Cellini Linecker*

What Color is Your Piggy Bank? Entrepreneurial Ideas for Self-Starting Kids
Text © 2004 Adelia Cellini Linecker
Illustrations © 2004 Sandra Lamb

Published by Lobster Press™
1620 Sherbrooke Street West, Suites C & D
Montréal, Québec   H3H 1C9
Tel. (514) 904-1100 • Fax (514) 904-1101 • www.lobsterpress.com

Publisher: Alison Fripp
Editors: Alison Fripp & Karen Li
Graphic Design & Production: Tammy Desnoyers

We acknowledge the financial support of the Government of Canada through the Book Publishing Industry Development Program (BPIDP) for our publishing activities.

The Canada Council | Le Conseil des Arts
for the Arts | du Canada

We acknowledge the support of the Canada Council for the Arts for our publishing program.

National Library of Canada Cataloguing in Publication

Cellini Linecker, Adelia, 1971-
    What color is your piggy bank? : entrepreneurial ideas for self-starting kids / Adelia Cellini Linecker.

ISBN 1-894222-82-2

    1. Money-making projects for children--Juvenile literature.
2. Entrepreneurship--Juvenile literature. I. Title.

HD62.5.C44 2004   j650.1'2   C2003-905944-8

Printed and bound in Canada.

TABLE OF CONTENTS

INTRODUCTION

MONEY. The root of all evil? Well it can be if you don't understand it properly. This book is going to help you learn how to earn money, save money and give money away (to charity) so that money works for you and not against you.

How many times have you heard your parents say, "Money doesn't just pop out of the ATM, you know." So where does it come from? Well, at your age, it comes from your parents who work hard to earn, save, and manage their money so they can provide for you and the rest of your family. In turn, you may earn an allowance for doing extra chores around the house, like washing the dishes or taking out the trash.

But what if you think your allowance is not enough, or you don't get one at all? How else can you get money to buy the things you need and want, fun things like CDs, DVDs, computer games, cell phones and MP3 players?

Now is the time to be creative and think outside the box. In other words, think of an idea that will earn you money. Be a young **entrepreneur**.

An entrepreneur is a person who creates, builds, and manages a business. It's a risky venture, one that's full of ups and downs, but in the end most successful entrepreneurs will tell you it's all worth it. You will have created a money-making job all your own, something that will interest and challenge you. And not only will you make some extra cash, you will also learn a lot about yourself, your desires, your skills, and your abilities.

What Color is Your Piggy Bank?

Entrepreneurial Ideas for Self-Starting Kids will guide you through all the steps to becoming a successful entrepreneur. Stuffed with tips, real-life stories, quizzes and an online connection to business starting templates, this book will show you, section by section, how to make and manage your money wisely.

Part I

The first step in creating your own work is to discover something that inspires you. What is inspiration? It is something that you are passionate about, interests you and makes you want to learn more. If you're passionate about your work, you'll not only earn money but you'll also enjoy your job. Tap into your creativity. Use your imagination. This section will give you great tips on how to give your idea all the energy it needs to make it succeed.

Part II

Establishing and maintaining an organized operation will keep your business running smoothly and your sanity intact! Section Two will give you the basics on how to set up shop.

Find out how to avoid getting buried in paperwork, keep a schedule, promote your business, team up with a partner, make your own tools, and estimate the cost of having your own business.

Part III

With some thought and hard work (and a little luck!) you'll be earning enough cash to start thinking about how you can spend some of it, too. This section will teach you how to manage your money. It will offer tips on how to save, spend and invest your hard-earned cash. From piggy banks to bank accounts to the basics of the stock market, you'll learn how to make your money work for you! As well, you'll look at ways you can use your money to make a difference in other people's lives by giving to charities and causes you're passionate about.

Truth be told, work is tough. You'll not only be required to invest a lot of your time and energy to get a business off the ground, but you'll also need a healthy dose of patience and persistence to make it keep working. So why be an entrepreneur at all? Many jobs that are hot today may become obsolete tomorrow. Think of bank tellers, airplane pilots and phone operators. Technology has replaced many of the functions that these jobs included. Take typesetting. Long before desktop publishing came onto the scene, people manually put together newsletters, newspapers, and other publications. Today, all that stuff is done on computers. Those typesetters who were savvy enough early on to explore and try out new ideas learned how to use desktop publishing. Those who didn't probably don't have a job today!

Learning to run your own business will arm you with the tools you need to succeed for the rest of your life. Now that's a tall order, so don't expect it to be all fun and games. But do remember to celebrate your successes – big and small!

Take the first step now and discover the world of jobs that awaits you!

Part I
THE WORLD OF JOBS

CHAPTER 1

Discover Your Talents and Interests

THERE are so many possibilities when it comes to work opportunities that it isn't always easy to know what you want to do. Some kids have their entire future mapped out and that's cool, but it's also an exception. For those of you who are unsure about what you want to do, just remember, it's never too early to start investigating your options. Think of it as a game of deduction. While there are numerous things you can do, your first task is to eliminate the choices that don't interest you. Here are some tips to help you narrow down your choices and figure out what kind of work would be perfect for you.

It might be helpful to arm yourself with a pen and notebook to keep track of your thoughts. Look for clues in all the things you do in a day. Ask yourself what you like to do in your spare time. Your **hobbies** are a good source of work ideas because you already know you enjoy doing those things. Go through the **chores** that you help

> *"Your work is to discover your work and then with all your heart give yourself to it."*
> **– Buddha**

out with around the house. If these things need to be done around your house, there's a good chance other people need the same chores done at their houses. Next, think about what you're good at in **school**. Are you a star athlete (or an aspiring one in gym class!)? Maybe you can coach younger kids in your neighborhood. If you enjoy art class, creating arts and crafts and selling them is an option you might consider.

IT'S NEVER TOO EARLY TO START PLANNING YOUR CAREER!

SKILLS FROM HOBBIES

Once you get a few ideas down on paper, think about the skills you use when you're doing those activities. Here's an example: Let's say your list of hobbies and things you enjoy doing includes arts and crafts, hanging out with friends and cooking. The skills involved in each of these things could include drawing, telling jokes, and baking cookies.

Put all of these talents together and you can be a party planner or helper. There are probably several moms in your neighborhood who could use your help in throwing a birthday party for their toddlers. You could offer to create banners and other party decorations, write up invitations, bake cookies and put together goody bags, and even play games with the kids.

The same list could produce a whole other set of skills, such as painting or sewing, bringing friends together, and organizing. How about opening up a mobile gift shop? Brainstorm and create great craft ideas with your friends and sell them at assisted living homes or convalescence hospitals. Add special touches to your creations like fresh flowers or baked goods. Visiting friends and families will appreciate the convenience of buying beautiful homemade gifts for their loved ones on the spot.

Sometimes it can be really challenging to find a way to turn your skills into job opportunities. If you're a book lover, you may think there's not much you can do to earn money while you read. Think again. As a great reader you can host a weekly story hour in your home (or in a shady spot in your yard!) for the kids in your neighborhood. If you're also a born entertainer, add more fun to story time by using puppets and acting out the stories. Parents will be

QUIZ ZONE

What Kind of Work Suits You?

There are tons of jobs out there and figuring out what kind of work best suits your talents and interests can be difficult. Take this quiz and get a better idea of what you might enjoy doing while earning some cash. Be honest with your answers; there are no right or wrong responses.

TURN TO THE END OF THE CHAPTER TO CHECK YOUR ANSWERS

1. *Working on school projects in a group is fun, even if sometimes you have to compromise to get the job done.*

   T or F

cont. on pg. 14

happy to pay for someone to look after and entertain their kids while they do their own chores.

Book lovers know a good story when they see one, and that's another important skill. Contact publishing houses and offer to review manuscripts for books aimed at your age group. For a fee, tell them you'll write up a detailed analysis of the story and a thorough review of why you liked the story or not.

SKILLS FROM CHORES

Some jobs involve doing stuff other people don't have time to do or simply don't like to do. The great thing about these jobs is that you already know how to do them! Why? The skills involved in these jobs you have already learned by doing chores around the house. By now you've probably had enough experience taking out the trash at your house that you can call yourself a sanitary expert. For a fee, you can bring your neighbors' garbage and recycling bins out to the curb before trash pickup day and return them after they've been emptied. For a little extra cash and some water fun, offer to hose out the containers.

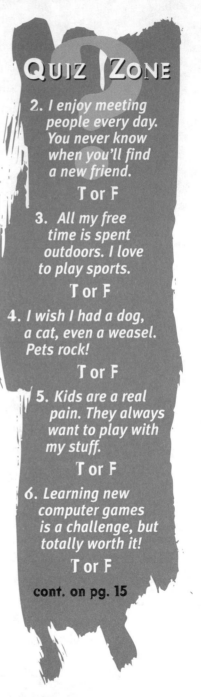

QUIZ ZONE

2. *I enjoy meeting people every day. You never know when you'll find a new friend.*

T or F

3. *All my free time is spent outdoors. I love to play sports.*

T or F

4. *I wish I had a dog, a cat, even a weasel. Pets rock!*

T or F

5. *Kids are a real pain. They always want to play with my stuff.*

T or F

6. *Learning new computer games is a challenge, but totally worth it!*

T or F

cont. on pg. 15

Put together a cleaning crew with a couple of your friends. There are tons of garages and tool sheds that need tidying up. Tell your neighbors you and your crew can organize screws and small tools in neatly separated boxes and drawers, sort out yard sale items, and paint a fence or garage door to complete the look.

Another idea: Many people also need help organizing things inside their homes. There isn't a house on earth that doesn't have a junk drawer or two in need of urgent sorting or a ton of loose change that can be wrapped in rolls. For a percentage of the money to be rolled, roll the coins and take them to the bank. These chore-related jobs are a great time to practice your people skills, remember, you can't pull a long face if you've offered to do other people's chores for money!

SKILLS FROM SCHOOL

Skills you've been learning at school can easily translate into job ideas. Take a look at your report card for inspiration. For instance, if kids you know aren't doing very well in your favorite subjects, they can benefit from your knowledge. How? If you're a math whiz, consider tutoring. You may never have taught before, but you'll never know how good you are unless you try it.

QUIZ ZONE

7. I am the chef of my home. I bake the best sugar cookies on earth.

T or F

8. I'm good at fixing things and making stuff with my hands.

T or F

TURN TO THE END OF THE CHAPTER ON PG. 21 TO CHECK YOUR ANSWERS

Start with tutoring one student for a couple of half hour sessions. Take it slow and take your time organizing your work. Being a tutor involves a lot of planning and progress tracking. First, you'll need to meet with your student and his or her parents to figure out what your student needs help with and to discuss how long it will take to get the kid up to speed. Together, you should plot out a timetable. Then, lessons will need to be prepared before each session. Finally, you should plan to send progress reports home to make sure the parents know how the lessons are going. If you can handle having one student for a while and feel you can add another one, don't be shy to ask your student to put the word out for you to his or her friends that you're available to tutor others who need help.

If you love art class, try making crafts and selling them at a local craft show or yard sale. Colorful magnets are always in high demand. Be creative about using materials you can get for free or cheap like funky-colored pebbles, seashells, and buttons. Use your imagination and save the earth, too, by collecting jars and cans from neighbors.

TRUE STORY

Tricks of the Trade

AMBER MCGRAW, 13, MONTARA, CALIFORNIA

Amber is not one to set her goals low. She dreams of taking a trip to Hawaii, where she'll stay at a fancy hotel, take hula lessons, and swim with dolphins. She knows this dream is an expensive one, so she's working hard to make it happen. She has three babysitting clients, is a pet-sitter for vacationing neighbors and teams up with her best friend to clean houses. So far, she's earned $500! And Amber knows that if her work is good, other referrals will come.

Classes at the local community center have prepared Amber as a babysitter; she brings her own bag of toys and games.

"Parents don't like it when their kids watch a lot of TV," she says. "And kids end up having more fun when you have stuff to play with." Some of her regular jobs come up when parents need an alternative to summer camp for their kids.

Summer is also a busy time for Amber's pet-sitting business. She takes care of the neighbor's cats when they're away on vacation. "I comb them, feed them and clean their litter box," says Amber. "I even teach them new tricks so the neighbors can see I took good care of them."

Amber also recently started house cleaning with her friend. One tip she has for earning a good wage and an excellent reputation is to write down everything you did to get the job done. For example, Amber and her friend swept, vacuumed, and cleaned out the kitchen sink. They even did some extra work, like dusting the wine cabinet. "When the lady read all the things we had done she paid each of us $7 an hour instead of $6!"

Clean them and decorate them to make personalized containers for coins, cookies, pens and pencils, and kitchen utensils.

Another option: Let parents in your neighborhood know that you can offer after-school arts and crafts lessons to their kids. For a fee, supply your students with basic materials and walk them through simple projects that you've learned at school. When their projects are finished, open a "gallery" in your backyard or driveway. You can make some extra money by charging for admission, and your students will also get the chance to have their masterpieces seen and sold.

Similarly, if you're good in sports, offer extra practice time to neighborhood kids who participate in community leagues. Plan round-robin tournaments to keep the competition level high and think of new practice drills to spice up the routine. The great thing about these kinds of jobs ideas is that parents will be happy to have some free time after work to prepare dinner, pay the bills, and tidy up the house.

Plus, their kids will get the chance to learn a lot from your skills and you get paid for taking care of them. It's a win-win situation.

Do you like acting? Do you participate in your school's drama club? If you're lucky enough to live in a city where a movie is being shot, you can be a movie extra. While acting experience is not always required, you do have to have some very important qualities. You must be extremely punctual and take the job seriously. No one likes a clown on the set who holds up production. And be ready to commit an entire day...or three. Being an extra can be slow-moving work. You can expect to wait around a lot, sometimes never being called into a scene.

Then even if you do make it into a scene, there's no guarantee that it won't end up on the cutting room floor.

On the other hand, the rewards can be huge: Not only can you earn up to $100 in a few days, you might even meet a movie star or two! You can find out about working as an extra by contacting casting agencies in your town. Also check out **www.moviextras.com** (you don't have to sign up as a paid member to get all the details). This site lets you create a resume and find local casting calls. It also offers links to other websites that have enough information to satisfy any movie buff or aspiring actor.

There are some jobs ideas that you may think up but are too young to do. Maybe you have a passion for writing and you dream of becoming a newspaper reporter. The fact of the matter is that you're going to have to go to school for a while longer before a newspaper will hire you. You'll need a work permit too, and in most cases you need to be 16 to get one. Does that mean you should give up on becoming a writer right now? Absolutely not. Your skills don't have to go to waste, you just have to be creative in applying them. You can come up with greeting card notes. If you have a flair for poetry, you can print some of your poems in greet-ing cards, too. Most computers come with software, such as Microsoft Publisher, that can help you design every aspect of your greeting card, from the way it folds to the font you use. You can also pick up greeting card paper and other fancy stationary at your local business supply store.

DEBBIE FIELDS (MRS. FIELDS COOKIES) DEVELOPED HER FIRST COOKIE RECIPE WHEN SHE WAS 13.

BILL GATES STARTED A SOFTWARE COMPANY WHEN HE WAS 15.

And don't just stop at greeting cards. Look at the words that exist around you. Someone had to come up with these slogans, ads, jokes and riddles. Take these ideas and make them your own. Create banners, pamphlets, flyers, bookmarks, and posters – whatever your clients desire! The point is this: No matter what skills you come up with, there will be a job idea that fits them. You just have to explore all opportunities from every possible angle to find the one that works for you.

Also take into consideration that whatever job idea you come up with, it's something you'll have to do over and over again. For example, if you plan to make and sell fudge, consider that you might have to spend hours in your kitchen-turned-fudge factory. You might get sick of the smell of chocolate by the end of the summer! The last thing you want to do is turn a hobby into a job you hate doing.

There are times when the work will seem tedious and you might feel like quitting. For example, you might love teaching kids a new language, but you're overwhelmed with the paperwork involved in tracking progress and preparing lessons. It would not only be rude to your students to quit tutoring, but also a setback for you as an entrepreneur. Part of being your own boss is having the discipline to focus on getting the job done – every part of the job, even if some of it is boring or difficult. The key is to remember that whatever you choose to do, you have to do it with all your heart.

QUIZ ZONE

Answers to Chapter 1 - What Kind of Work Suits You?

If you answered...

1. **T =** Start a partnership with one or two of your friends. But understand that there are tradeoffs when working with others. What does this mean? Pretend you and your best friend start a business where you run errands for the elderly or new moms in your neighborhood on Saturdays. The good part is that you can work while hanging out with your friends. But what if you have a fight at school? It might be awkward to work with your friend, but you still have to honor the commitment you both made to your customers.

F = You like to make your own decisions and set your own timetable. If you'd rather be playing soccer at the park in the afternoon and leave the craft work for evening, that's no problem because you didn't promise anyone you'd be working during the day. Of course, everyone needs help sometimes, so don't be shy to ask a friend to help you if you're having a bake sale, for example.

2. T = Your work should include meeting as many people as you can – like a party planner. If you like to play with younger kids and enjoy teaching them new games, try babysitting. To meet kids your age, try setting up a veggie stand or a car wash station in front of your house. One way or another, you're bound to meet interesting people – and earn some money at the same time!

F = Part of every job involves meeting new people. But if you don't like to spend much face time with people you don't really know, you might think of jobs that you can do in your home. Are you a wordsmith? After the initial effort to get the word out that you're a good writer, you can work solo writing greeting cards in the comfort of your own home!

3. T = Well, this is a no-brainer. If you enjoy the outdoors so much, work outside! Ask your neighbors if they'll hire you to do yard work. But think beyond the obvious, too. Are you a star tennis player? Let parents around the neighborhood know that you can offer tennis classes to younger kids. You can do this for just about any sport.

F = While it's a good idea to spend some time outdoors, you prefer to work inside. Think of jobs that you can do at your house or someone else's house. Are you a neat person? Maybe there's a new mom in your neighborhood that could use some help tidying up on weekends. Or you can lend a hand to an elderly couple that needs to have their recyclables collected around the house and taken to the curb once a week.

4. T = There are several different jobs for animal lovers from dog walking to cat-sitting to setting up a dog wash in your front yard. Think outside the box and find out if neighbors have pets you don't know about like goldfish, hamsters, turtles, and even snakes! All of them need care when their owners can't be around. So go ahead and let them know you're available to help.

F = OK, so you don't really want to scoop doggie messes for a few bucks, but there are a lot of people in your neighborhood with pets. Do you like making arts and crafts? Try your hand at making and selling personalized pet dishes, leashes and dog sweaters. There are job opportunities all around you. The key is to take the time and look at your situation from different angles. By thinking of solutions in a new way, you may come up with work ideas that are interesting to you and in demand.

5. T = You're better suited to working for adults. Offer to do some handy work that you're able and allowed to do. Maybe clean out someone's garage and offer to organize shelves and drawers. If you live in a place where it snows in winter, you can make some money shoveling snow from walkways and driveways.

F = Besides babysitting, those of you who love kids have a host of other job prospects. You can offer to help parents plan kids' birthday parties, tutor their little ones in reading or walk their kids to and from school. Other ideas: Host a story hour each week at your house or set up a babysitting area at neighborhood parties so parents can mingle without worrying about the kids.

6. T = You were born to work with computers. Use your talents to teach other kids, or even grown-ups, how to use computers. Another way to use your computer savvy to make a few dollars is to offer to publish and sell newsletters, party invitations and banners to local clubs.

F = Maybe you don't know very much about computers. Hey, it's never too late to learn! Do you have a buddy who's a techno-whiz? Team up and learn to use a computer in exchange for your skills in a subject your friend could use some help with.

7. **T =** Bake sales, refreshment stands, veggie counters – you name it, you can sell it if it tastes good. Besides setting up a stand in front of your house, you can increase your business by setting up shop at yard sales and car washes. You might even think about starting a catering service for birthday parties and PTA meetings.

   F = You may not like baking and cooking, but there's always a lot of non-cooking work to be done at a party. Examples? Help out with food and drink deliveries, set up the buffets, keep the ice cooler full, and pick up trash. If you're great at organizing, or smart with money, your buddy who likes to cook and bake might also need a hand keeping track of orders and collecting payment from clients.

8. **T =** There's work for you in just about any neighborhood. If you're good at repairing bikes, let neighborhood kids know that for a small fee you can fix a flat tire or replace a chain. Are you good with your hands in an artistic way? Try making beaded necklaces and bracelets that you can sell either on your own or as part of a yard sale.

   F = You're creative but not so hot on the mechanical stuff. There are still plenty of ways to work with your hands. Consider offering gardening services. Some people will want to just buy tulip bulbs from you and plant them themselves. Others might want you to get your own hands in the dirt, too!

CHAPTER 2

Do You Have What It Takes?

THINKING up a great job idea will take you one step closer to your dream of bringing in the big bucks for the things you need and want, but there is more to being an entrepreneur than *dreaming* up ways to make money. It's time to make a plan and execute your idea. How can you be sure that people will want to hire you or that they will want your products? There are four important ingredients to being a successful entrepreneur: **curiosity**, **creativity**, **flexibility**, and **commitment**. With these four things in mind, you will be able to take your passions and put them into a successful action plan, one that will have clients coming back for more. Follow the tips below to help you strengthen these four traits in yourself and in your business.

✓ CURIOSITY

✓ CREATIVITY

✓ FLEXIBILITY

✓ COMMITMENT

CURIOSITY

Curiosity means looking at the world around you and taking note of what's been done, what hasn't been done, and what could be done better. Successful entrepreneurs know what people want and move quickly to deliver it. How do they know what people want? When companies try to find out if people want their services and products they do **market research**. This can include phone calling a specific set of people, or a **focus group**, and asking them a range of questions from what they like, dislike and want, to what they think of the company's products and services. Market research can also be done through surveys and sample offerings.

> *"Think left and think right and think low and think high. Oh, the thinks you can think up if you only try!"*
> **– Dr. Seuss (Theodor Geisel)**

Of course, you don't have to do all of these things – it would take you years to complete and analyze all the research! You can try some of the strategies on a smaller scale. Use your natural **curiosity** to see what people want and need. Some people call it having your finger on the pulse. That's just a fancy way of saying you are aware of the trends. How do you get to know what the trends are? Talk to people, observe what they do, read books and magazines, listen to the radio and watch television. Ask lots of questions, and more importantly, listen to the answers.

Think about how you're going to do market research. Let's say you want to start a birthday party catering business in your neighborhood. You're thinking about baking delicious desserts you know all kids love. Estimate how many kids under eight years old are in your neighborhood. If there are too few kids, then you'll have a hard time finding clients. Then find out how many other people are already catering to kids' parties. Check the Yellow Pages to see if there are professional services available. You wouldn't want to waste your time and money setting up a baking business only to find out that there are dozens of other people already doing the same thing.

Market research helps companies figure out not only what people think of their products but of rivals' products as well. When companies get the scoop on how the competition is faring, they can offer a better service or product. You don't have to gather people for a focus group, but think of some questions you can use as a survey for parents who have hired party planners before. What did they like about hiring the professional service? What did they dislike? Would they consider buying baked goods from you if you threw in nicely wrapped cookies as party favors? What other extras would entice them away from your competitors?

CREATIVITY

Once you know enough to decide that it's worth starting your business, you need **creativity** to come up with ways to make your business stand out from the rest. Your cookies, cakes and other baked goods have to be first rate. And your personalized service has to make them want to contract with you rather than Dairy Queen or Costco, who make individualized birthday cakes for rock-bottom prices as low as $16.

Your attention to their individual needs will set you apart from the rest. Maybe you have a special way of presenting the cookies you bake, or you include serving the food at the party as an option. Take this idea a step further and offer to help set up the food table and clean up after the party. Perhaps your research shows that parents would like party planners to combine catering and entertainment. Team up with a friend who's a great entertainer. Take that idea of extra services up a notch and get together with someone who has their life-saving certificate who can supervise kids at a pool party. Maybe other planners don't

QUIZ ZONE

Who Am I?

Circle the response that you can most relate to. If you cannot decide between two options, you can circle both. Remember, there are no wrong answers!

TURN TO THE END OF THE CHAPTER TO CHECK YOUR ANSWERS

1. When your bike gets busted:
   A. *I discover ways to fix it.*
   B. *I think up ways to build a better bike.*
   C. *Taxi!*
   D. *Man, I've had that bike forever!*

2. Style Watch:
   A. *I can spot a trend before you'd even know it was cool.*
   B. *I hate looking like everyone else, so I make my own style.*

cont. on pg. 29

decorate. Your service can provide theme-oriented decorations depending on the child's likes and dislikes.

If you're competing with other kids who are running a similar business, use your creativity to think up extra special ways to stand out with your professionalism. Make use of your computer to create eye-catching business cards with all your contact information, provide an easy-to-read reference sheet of satisfied customers, print memorable pamphlets with a list of services and extras that you can offer. (*Check out more on promotional tools in Chapter 9!*) There are also plenty low-tech ways to stand out. For instance, it helps to always be neat in appearance and polite. Saying please and thank you is the simplest way to be polite and ensure that you make a good impression on customers who might refer you to their friends.

FLEXIBILITY

One of the greatest advantages to creating your own job is that you can adapt your ideas to the possibilities that exist around you. This is called **flexibility**. Larger companies tend to move more slowly when it comes to following new trends; they have

QUIZ ZONE

C. I adapt the clothing I see to suit my personal look.

D. I wear one outfit, 24/7.

3. If my best friend got dumped, the first thing I'd say is:

A. Why?

B. You can do so much better.

C. Let me introduce you to my cousin.

D. But I thought you loved one another!

4. My computer just crashed, so I'm going to:

A. Research what went wrong.

B. Push a few buttons to see if it comes back to life. If not, reboot the system.

C. Work on my laptop.

D. Send the big box out for repairs.

cont. on pg. 30

QUIZ ZONE

5. You and your bud can't agree on which flick to rent:

A. Try to see what your friend likes in her movie picks.

B. Forget the movie idea. You decide to have a games night.

C. Let her chose the movie this time and agree that you get to pick next time.

D. You really want to see your movie choice, so you rent both and have a weekend movie marathon with your bud!

TURN TO THE END OF THE CHAPTER ON PG. 35 TO CHECK YOUR ANSWERS

many clients and must cater to their common needs. If a larger company were to suddenly change what they offer, many clients would simply jump ship to another provider. In contrast, smaller companies have fewer clients and can cater to their needs on a one-on-one basis; they are quicker on their feet to fill new demands. The result? Their clients tend to stick around as long as the smaller company can help them with their changing needs in a timely fashion. Think of the comparison as two trucks trying to make a turn. A large 18-wheeler has to take it slow and easy in order to avoid a jack-knife accident. A smaller pickup truck can zip right through!

For instance, if you're still offering to deck out the party scene with the Mighty Morphin Power Rangers, you might be a little dated. Kids today are looking forward to the next install-ment of the Spider-man movie. Keep your eyes and ears open for new things that people are discovering. Are there sports or recreational activities that are more popular this summer than they were last year? Is there a fashion fad that you can turn into a job idea?

How can you incorporate these new trends into what your business already offers? If you are already catering kids' parties and you notice that hair wraps are totally hot this season, learn how to do them. Then you can set up an area at your party where kids pay extra to get their hair wrapped up in crazy colors! If you know your neighbor's kids are really into basketball, offer not only your babysitting services, but after-school basketball practice, too. Flexibility means that you can adapt to the changing demands of your clients. The most successful entrepreneurs never go out of style!

Being flexible also means being ready to change your ideas and adapt your plans as you encounter obstacles along the way. Let's say you've come up with the most zany, mouthwatering Popsicle flavors. Before you set up a Popsicle stand on your front lawn, think about how you're going to keep those frozen delights, well, frozen?

Will you have to keep running inside to get more Popsicles every time you run out? Who will look after your cash box while you do that? So now you have two things to consider: Do you have all the tools to make your business work? And is this a job that you can do alone, or is it better if you ask a friend to become a partner? One way to do it is to have a really good cooler and keep your Popsicles right under the table. Another solution is to team up with a friend and you can take turns running back inside the house to get more Popsicles. Either way, you have to be ready to adapt your original idea to problems that may arise. If you don't, your business might flop before it has a good chance of getting started. And that's no fun at all.

COMMITMENT

Now it's time to follow through and bring your ideas to life. This may be the hardest part of running your business – **staying committed** to your plans. It's going to take a lot of time and energy to get your idea off the ground. People have to hear about what a great job you do, so there's a lot of work in spreading the word before you even get a job. You may not even make a profit from your first job because of **startup costs**. These expenses include tools you need to buy to get the job done, money you have to spend to get the word out, and other costs related to improving your skills. For a catering service, there will be startup costs like buying cooking utensils and ingredients. You might consider buying a cookbook to add new ideas to your menu. If you use flyers to advertise your business, think about the costs of stationary, too. In fact, you'll probably have to get another client or two before you make some money. Hang in there and it will pay off in the end!

Commitment also means running your business responsibly; make sure you have the time and energy to fulfill promises. If this is a business you want to do year-round, consider if it will interfere with your schoolwork. Remember, your goal is to finish what you start. If you need extra training to run your business properly, factor in the time it will take to do that, too. For instance, you'll have to carve out time to practice new recipes if you start a catering business. If you offer gardening services, you may have to take some time to research the kinds of plants you'll be dealing with, and how to best take care of them.

Being on time is also important in keeping your promises to clients. If you tell someone you're going to be at their house to help set up the buffet before the party starts, be there when you say you will, if not a little earlier. That means you'll have to be careful about how you schedule your other activities. Don't give up your entire life for your business, but be sure to give yourself enough time to get from, say, soccer practice to the party you're helping to cater.

People used to save cash in kitchen jars made of a clay called pygg and called them pygg jars. Later they became known as "piggy banks" and made in the shape of pigs.

Last but not least, stay committed to yourself and your ideas. Have the courage to believe in yourself even when others may doubt you. It's OK to listen to others and ask for their opinions. Some people may be offering advice because they have experience. Maybe they've already tried to run a catering business. Listening to them can help you avoid making some mistakes. But don't be afraid to make mistakes either. Some things you just have to learn on your own; you'll discover how to do things better the next time around. Think of it as market research through experience.

Remember, there will be difficult times but challenges make the journey interesting and the rewards that much sweeter! Besides, the only way that you will find out if your brilliant ideas are worth anything at all is to put them in motion, right? Then you will truly find out if you have what it takes to be a successful young entrepreneur.

QUIZ ZONE

Answers to Chapter 2 - Who Am I?

If you answered...

MOSTLY A'S

Thanks to your eagle-eye surveillance of everything around you, you will always be in the know. **Curiosity** is your greatest strength and as an entrepreneur you will have no problems figuring out what your clients want. **BEWARE:** Don't be afraid to take your curiosity a step further and think up your own great ideas. Keeping your eyes peeled for trends is one thing, taking action and putting your ideas to work is another. Go ahead and take the plunge. Then take it up another notch and stick to your decisions.

MOSTLY B'S

You can come up with a fix for just about anything. And the solutions can be out of this world. Your **creativity** allows you to look at problems from several different angles. By analyzing many ways to get a job done, you're constantly trying to improve – a key to entrepreneurial success. **CAUTION:** You don't have to rely on yourself alone for all the answers. You can ask others around you for help. Be flexible and have an open mind. You never know when someone has a better solution to offer.

MOSTLY C'S

No chance of you becoming obsolete! You're **flexible** and understand that things change all the time. Your ability to go with the flow means you'll be able to better serve your clients' needs as they change. <u>RED FLAG</u>: Don't be so flexible that you can be convinced to do just about anything. Stick to principles you set for yourself. A couple wants you to baby-sit their kid, but they routinely come back two hours after they say they'll be home? If you've already charged them extra a couple of times and asked them not to be late again (especially on a school night!), then you've been flexible enough. Politely tell them you're not available.

MOSTLY D'S

You're a rock and you will not be moved. Your **commitment** is a key entrepreneurial trait because you'll need all the determination you can muster to stick to your business plans and make them succeed. Many entrepreneurs face doubt, from within and from others. A strong commitment ensures that you stay the course until a job is done. <u>WARNING</u>: Being too narrow in your focus can cause you to miss the big picture. It's great that you're committed to doing things your way, but it's OK to tinker with smaller decisions along the way. You may find ideas that make your work more efficient.

Chapter 3
Training Camp!

BY now, you've discovered your passions, you've thought up some great job ideas, and you've figured out what it takes to be a great entrepreneur. What's next? Now you might want to spend some time making sure you can make good on your promises to your clients. If you constantly strive to improve and update your skills, you can be sure you're keeping up with what you're expected to know about your job. Successful entrepreneurs know that learning is constant.

Knowing how to do your job to the best of your abilities is good for two reasons. First, you'll feel more confident about your skills, and that will help you do your job more easily. Second, once your clients see that they can trust your abilities, they will feel more comfortable giving you more responsibilities. In their eyes, you can be counted on to do the job well.

Imagine you're looking for babysitting work. You might have experience babysitting your little sister or a cousin. That's

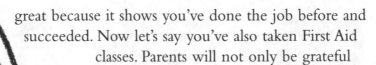

great because it shows you've done the job before and succeeded. Now let's say you've also taken First Aid classes. Parents will not only be grateful that you'll entertain their kids, but they'll also appreciate your safety savvy. There are several places where you can sign up for CPR or First Aid classes. The best places to attend these classes (and where they are often offered for free) are your local YMCA and YWCA and your local chapter of the Red Cross. You'll learn everything from putting a Band-Aid on a scraped knee to how to perform CPR or the Heimlich maneuver on a small child.

Sometimes these places will offer baby-sitting classes where you'll be taught the basics of caring for kids, from changing diapers to making easy meals. You'll also learn how to tell stories, play games and make crafts appropriate for the kid's age. As well, classes can help you understand children's behavior by teaching a bit about child psychology so that you'll know what to do if the little angel you're looking after suddenly has a meltdown. It will be helpful to have some coping skills rather than sit there with a screaming child for hours. You'll learn why some kids need a certain amount of attention, what they will do to get it, and how you should respond to it. In many cases, you may have to discipline the child even though you're not the parent. Classes will offer tips on how to be firm yet kind when you follow the parents' guidelines (they know their kid best). On the flipside, it's also important to know how to be friendly while still maintaining your status as the person in charge. It's a balancing act that babysitting classes can help you achieve.

If you've decided to sell crafts at yard sales or stationary at school, you might consider looking for ways to improve your creative skills. Arts and crafts classes can teach you new crafting ideas and how to work with different materials. You'll come out of these lessons with fresh ideas for new products that can expand your offerings to clients. Art supplies stores usually set aside a day a week to invite kids to try their hand at making new crafts. Look for art classes at museums and kids' stores like Gymboree, too. Even some Home Depot stores offer classes, which include craft and woodworking activities for youngsters.

"It's not that I'm so smart, it's that I stay with problems longer."
– Albert Einstein

Local fabric stores often give sewing lessons, too. But be sure the classes are meant for kids. You'll learn how to use a sewing machine to make hair scrunchies, pillowcases, aprons, quilts, boxers and pyjamas. Some classes teach you how to choose the fabric with

INTERNET INSIGHTS

the right texture for a specific project. You may even improve skills you already have. You know how to sew in a straight line, but are rounded edges giving you trouble? These classes can help make your creations look more professional, making it more likely that they will fetch you more money!

Where do inventors go to get bulb-lighting ideas? Why, they go to engineering camp! You can spend part of your summer making new toys and the rest of it selling them. Elementary schools often host these camps in summertime, and many science centers and museums house them through-out the year. Use your creativity to design and invent toys and prepare a marketing and sales plan.

Other camps offer places for computer and math whizzes to learn more of what they love. Many of the things you learn at these camps are also useful if you're going to tutor others. Example: Say you invent a computer game that forces you to use your math skills to win a race. Why not use this game to tutor a kid in math?

Community centers are good places to join dance and music classes. Look for classes that teach you how to use props and instruments you've never used before. These skills will make you a smash hit as a party entertainer. It can even make you a star some day! J.Lo learned to dance at the Kips Bay Boys and Girls Club in the Bronx. In addition to community centers, shop around local theaters for acting lessons. These classes can make you a better storyteller.

Expand your menu with cooking classes. You might bake the tastiest oatmeal cookies, but you will want to offer other delicious delights when you start your catering service. Cooking classes can teach you basic skills like handling a knife, sauté work, poaching, roasting and more. Learn to make quick and easy one-pot meals like pot roast and chicken potpies. If you're thinking of working through the winter, learning to make chill-buster soups like vegetable mine-strone and chicken soup is a must.

Get down and dirty with garden-ing classes at botanical gardens and local greenhouses. You'll learn about soil, veg-etables, insects, worms, watering and more. If you're already a hobby gardener, take some advanced classes that will expand your knowledge about caring for lawns

www.redcross.ca

FIND YOUR LOCAL RED CROSS LOCATION AND ASK ABOUT SAFETY CLASSES LIKE CPR AND FIRST AID.
IN THE U.S. GO TO:

www.redcross.org

www.homedepot.com

LOCATE THE HOME DEPOT NEAREST YOU AND CHECK OUT IF THEY'RE OFFERING CRAFTS AND WOOD-WORKING CLASSES. REMEMBER, YOU CAN ALSO GO TO CRAFT STORES AND YOUR LOCAL COMMUNITY CENTER FOR ART CLASSES.

www.ctcnet.org

THIS IS A NATIONAL NON-PROFIT MEMBERSHIP ORGANIZATION OF MORE THAN 1,000 INDEPENDENT COMMUNITY TECHNOLOGY CENTERS WHERE PEOPLE GET FREE OR LOW-COST ACCESS TO COMPUTERS AND RELATED TECHNOLOGY, SUCH AS THE INTERNET, TOGETHER WITH LEARNING OPPORTUNITIES.

www.schoolnet.ca

FIND TONS OF INFORMATION ON JOB TRAINING, SURVEYS AND THE INTERNET.

www.ja.org

JUNIOR ACHIEVEMENT'S WEBSITE IS A COOL TOOL TO GET EDUCATED ABOUT BUSINESS, ECONOMICS AND FREE ENTERPRISE.

and gardens. There are always new products on the market to make lawns greener and weeds disappear. Be the first to know about them and then try to sell them to your clients. The latest trends cater to people who want to grow organic fruits and vegetables. Find out what it means to have an organic garden and which products you can and can't use to keep produce organic. Armed with this knowledge you can go after even the most sophisticated client.

Some community centers have classes specifically to improve your people skills, which are important in just about any job. Look for leadership classes that offer tips on how to work in groups, make difficult decisions, and improve your communications skills. Business etiquette classes can show you how to behave professionally around adults and earn their respect and confidence.

Entrepreneurs, being a self-starting bunch of people, also improve their skills on their own.

You can do the same – right at home! If you have a computer, there are tons of software programs that can help sharpen your skills. There are programs that teach you to type faster, multiply your math skills, and expand your vocabulary to read and write with more ease. Even if you're a computer whiz, there's always room for improvement. Maybe you'd like to learn how to create web pages. Look for software that teaches you to use HTML (that's the programming language used to create web pages). Doing your own research and training at home has the added perk of learning on your own schedule and at your own pace.

The Internet is an awesome research tool as well. From published articles to websites to discussion boards, you can surf the Internet to learn about new trends and talk to others to find out if they have a solution to a problem. Have you tried everything you know about how to get Photoshop to crop a picture a certain way but failed? Search the web for a message board that lets you ask for help from other Photoshop users. Chances are someone out there will have come across the same issue and figured out a solution.

Bookstores and libraries are also great places to do research. Read up on activities you're interested in. Scan for books on job ideas like gardening and jewelry making. You can even pick up a songbook to learn the lyrics of some of kids' favorite songs. Once you've learned them, you can sing them to a group of kids at a party or to the toddler you're babysitting. Many bookstores and libraries even offer story hours; if you are unsure of what younger kids are reading nowadays, stop by to find out. You can also pick up great tips on how to keep children captivated by your storytelling.

Extra training can also come from volunteering. Sure, there's no pay involved, but the rewards are nevertheless huge. Future employers will see that you are capable of being passionate about what you do regardless of pay. Your pride in your work and understanding of the importance of charity in a community will show that you appreciate the social value of work. You don't just work to make big bucks; you work because your job also makes a difference in people's lives.

Find a group that offers activities that interest you. By joining clubs like the Scouts or community groups that help feed the poor or care for the elderly and disabled, you'll learn leadership and organizational skills that can help in any job. Bonus: Working with people of different ages and backgrounds will offer tips on how to cooperate with others. Learning to cooperate, organize, and negotiate can be key in dealing with customers and coworkers (in case you start a business with a friend or two).

Upgrading your skills shouldn't be a chore. While learning new tricks of the trade isn't always easy, especially when you're trying to master complex skills, your desire to be a great entrepreneur should be a strong motivation. Getting better at what you like and finding new and better ways to do it not only helps you do your job better but also adds to the goods and services you can offer people. In the process, you may even meet new people (who can become new clients or partners).

CHAPTER 4
New Twists on Traditional Jobs

AS you learn more skills, you can think of ways to put new twists on traditional jobs. Adding extra services to your business will change the pace and help you earn a little extra money. Other times the challenge comes from adapting your services so that they are offered throughout the year instead of just during the summer. If you tweak your ideas just a touch, you'll be surprised by what you can offer and how much more fun it can be.

Take babysitting. There are several ways to make babysitting a little different. By offering your services for different occasions, you'll expand your client base. Think of when parents might need your help. The first thing that pops into your mind is to offer babysitting services to parents who have to go to a party or dinner. That's a good idea. But parents also need help when they're right there in the house. When parents come home from work, they usually need time to make dinner and prepare lunches for the next day. Bingo! You can be there for an hour or so before dinner so they can get their chores done. Another idea: Many parents work from home and would pay you a good wage to entertain their kid while they got some extra work done. Ask your parents if they know anyone in the neighborhood who works from home. New moms are also in need of this kind of service even if they're not working from home. They may need to get chores done or make a grocery run while you watch the baby.

Some babysitting jobs are as easy as taking a walk. Offer to walk younger kids to and from school, the bus stop, ballet classes, etc. You can also supervise kids at the park while parents watch a baseball game or a soccer match. Bring some art supplies along and set up an area where you can paint faces and make simple crafts. You can use this set up at barbecues and yard sales, too.

Holidays also are a good time to expand your babysitting services.

QUIZ ZONE

Are You A Born Entrepreneur?

Look at the list of characteristics below and give yourself a score from 1 to 5 (1 = strongly disagree and 5 = strongly agree) for each statement. Then tally up your score and see if you were born to start your own business or if you need a little help before diving into entrepreneurship.

TURN TO THE END OF THE CHAPTER TO CHECK YOUR SCORE

1. I am passionate about important things.

score from 1 to 5

2. I often come up with creative ways to solve problems.

score from 1 to 5

cont. on pg. 47

QUIZ ZONE

3. I am confident that I can accomplish what I set out to do.

score from 1 to 5

4. I appreciate help from others, but I rely on myself to get the job done.

score from 1 to 5

5. I'm competitive and I like to work hard to learn new skills.

score from 1 to 5

6. I think ahead to avoid problems and get new ideas.

score from 1 to 5

7. I'm not afraid to try a new idea if I've thought it through.

score from 1 to 5

TURN TO THE END OF THE CHAPTER ON PG. 53 TO CHECK YOUR SCORE

Grown-ups need extra time to plan holiday parties, make food, and buy presents. You can adapt the holidays into your activities. At Easter, teach kids how to paint and dye their own eggs. Then set up an Easter egg hunt in your front yard. Put on your thinking cap and hide colorful eggs in sneaky little places like inside the mailbox. At Halloween, help younger kids make costumes and then take them trick-or-treating. During the Christmas season, spend an afternoon having the kids make Christmas ornaments or a small present for their parents while their mom or dad is doing their last minute Christmas shopping.

There are other ways to add a little zest to the babysitting idea. Help kids with their homework rather than just baby-sit them. If you're good at a certain subject, like math, tell the moms in your neighborhood that you'd be happy to go over their child's math homework while you're babysitting. Don't forget to pack your materials like counting beads, exercise books, rulers, pens, and pencils. Parents will appreciate, and perhaps be willing to pay more for, your offering two services in one.

Other jobs that could use a little twist? Kids have been mowing lawns almost since grass was invented. Dig a little deeper and put your green thumb to better use. Think of your business as a lawn-and-garden service. Some people may be afraid to let you use a large, electric lawn mower, so offer to rake leaves, water lawns and flower gardens, pull weeds from a vegetable garden, and remove snow in winter time. Most homes also have backyard sheds that could use a cleanup once in a while.

And don't limit yourself to the backyard. Elderly neighbors and new moms in your neighborhood will truly appreciate you running simple errands for them. Ask if they would like you to take their trash to the curb on a weekly basis and pick up a copy of the weekend paper or a favorite magazine if they don't have a subscription. If there's a convenience store right around the corner, you can offer to pick up some groceries like bread and milk. Other errands you can help out with include picking up dry cleaning items and taking mail and special parcels to the post office.

Summer months are a great time to offer services to neighbors who are away on vacation. Most insurance companies insist that someone go into the house every few days at least, so you can start with that. You can also go to collect their mail if they don't have it stopped; overstuffed mailboxes are a tell-tale sign for burglars that no one is home. Do they have pets, too? Though homeowners usually send dogs to kennels, some will leave their cats behind and need someone to feed and change their litter daily. Indoor plants will also need regular watering while your neighbors are gone. Find out who's going on vacation and ask them if they need you to take care of their home while they're away.

Even for those neighbors who are staying close to home, summertime help is always welcome. Do they have pools that need cleaning? Outdoor furniture, sheds, porches, and decks all need painting at least once a year. If you do a good job in the summer, you can remind your neighbors that you're also available during winter holidays should they be out of town.

Dog walking is another all-time favorite. Neighbors who are on vacation or at work during the day are potential clients. There are other pets that need care. Cats, birds, hamsters all need to be fed and cared for. Maybe you know of a pet that needs special attention because it recently had a surgery or is recovering from an accident. Offer to check up on the pet and call the owner if there's anything wrong. If you have the experience and are really good with animals, start a pet-care service. Earn extra cash by cleaning bird and hamster cages and giving cats and dogs a bath.

Doing odd jobs around the neighborhood allows you to do different things for different people. There's never a boring moment if you provide different services depending on what people need. Besides, assisting people in your community will help spread the word that you're a competent and reliable worker. Good word-of-mouth will earn you solid references and additional clients.

Let's take another traditional job and think of new ways to do it. Bake sales are a kid favorite, but pretty common, so you'll have to find ways to make your business stand out. Did you ever think of making care packages for people to send to friends and family? Create a different package for every theme. Bring along samples of your package decorations and have customers choose which one they want. For example, a mom might choose to personalize her package with baseball bats and catcher's mitts for her son who's on the varsity baseball team in college. Write "Get Well" in cheerful colors on a package of cookies going to someone who is under the weather. Use stickers with apples and "A+" signs on them on a package for a special teacher.

INTERNET INSIGHT

www.youngbiz.com

THIS IS A COLORFUL WEBSITE WITH AN ENCYCLOPEDIA'S WORTH OF INFO FOR YOUNG ENTREPRENEURS ALONG WITH A BUNCH OF TRUE STORIES TO INSPIRE YOU TO TRY YOUR HAND AT STARTING A NEW BUSINESS.

Don't limit your products to obvious markets. Who else could benefit from your baking skills? Why not try your hand at making animal treats like dog biscuits? You'll have to do some research and maybe check out the bookstore or go on the web to look for recipes, but it'll probably be worth your time and effort. Sure, people can get their pet treats at the store. But if you offer to make them with, say, natural ingredients and guarantee that they're made fresh and delivered that morning, you might have a leg up on the competition! Did you know that Americans and Europeans spend $17 billion a year on pet food!

If you're an entrepreneur, you better hope you don't have Chematophobia. Why? Uh, because that's the fear of money!

New ideas can also come from combining two tried-and-true jobs. For example, car washing and a refreshment stand make a good pair. Team up with a friend and cool your feet while making some cash. How does this work? When people are waiting around in the hot sun to get their car washed, offer a refreshing glass of lemonade! Use one business to feed customers to the other one.

Party planners can also offer a cleaning service. Say you're hired to be a clown at a kids' birthday party. Once the party's over, you can make a quick costume change, throw on some sweat pants and help clean up toys and other items.

Need some more quick ideas on how to spice up a traditional job? Check out the appendix: "Jobs in a Nutshell" at the back of this book. Each tip sheet has innovative ideas on how to give any business a twist and troubleshoot problems before they even arise.

Of course, more work means added responsibilities. If you're offering more services, you'll have to plan carefully and make sure you don't stretch yourself too thin. There's no point in saying you'll do more if the quality of your work suffers. Clients will remember that you did a bad job and you'll probably end up with less work and more stress. You'll also have to be focused and motivated to do your job for longer stretches of time. There will be more distractions if you work during school, like class trips, parties, and varsity sports. Your commitment will be tested. Be sure you've balanced work, school, and extracurricular activities at levels that you can sustain throughout the year.

If you do it right, your ability to **multitask** – or to do more than one thing at a time – will impress your clients and possibly lead to more work, too. Trying out new ideas is also an important part of running a business. When you have an open mind, there are many ideas that can add a little pizzazz to your job. People's needs change all the time. If you're aware of these trends, you'll be better able to respond to them.

Quiz Zone

Answers to Chapter 4 -
Are You A Born Entrepreneur?

If you scored...

BIZZY BODY: 30-35 POINTS

You're wired to be an entrepreneur. Your confidence, creativity, and passion are great assets in the business world. In fact, you probably already have tons of ideas that could turn into successful businesses. But be careful not to get overwhelmed with the seemingly endless possibilities. You're very talented and it's possible that more than one of your ideas could turn into a great business. But focus on one or two, which is probably as much as you can handle while still having fun.

BIZ INTERN: 20-30 POINTS

You know the basics of what it takes to be a successful entrepreneur. Now you need to take it to the next level and really understand all the details. Read up on some of the things you're not sure about. Talk to people you look up to and ask them if they have any answers to your questions. Is there a mentor or a role model you can look to for advice?

It's OK not to know everything. Learning is part of the process of becoming a smart businessperson.

BIZ ALERT!: LESS THAN 20 POINTS

Your interest in starting your own business is impressive. And kudos to you for thinking about striking out on your own. But you have a lot to learn and that can be overwhelming. Don't give up. Ask your parents to help you through the process. They can help you think about what business best suits your goals and skills. They can even suggest ways to learn some of the key skills you need to run a successful business. Hey, everyone needs to start somewhere, so do some research, plan your goals, and go for it!

Part II
SETTING UP SHOP

CHAPTER 5
Making a Schedule

ONE of the biggest mistakes kids make when they start their own businesses is underestimating the amount of time they will spend working. Sure, there's plenty of fun in doing something you're passionate about and enjoy. But there's a difference between having fun while you work and just plain chilling. On the other hand, you don't want to spend all your time working without having time to enjoy the money you make. If you want to make sure your business is successful, you'll have to spend some time planning. It is important to find a good balance between work and play.

The best way to figure out how to balance work and free time is to make a schedule. Making a schedule is as easy as jotting down on a calendar all the activities and chores you are already dedicated to doing. It's a helpful exercise because, off the top of your head, it is actually quite easy to have some activities slip your mind. Schedules are a great way to jog your memory and visually plot out your availability.

Once you have a schedule down on paper, you can easily calculate how much time you can dedicate to your new work. If you're just starting out, devoting ten hours a week to your new job is ideal. Think of it in terms of working weekends and maybe a couple hours a day during the week. But remember, if you're planning on working all year long, a big chunk of your time should be dedicated to school and homework.

One more point: It's a good idea to share your schedule with your parents. Why? They can offer tips and advice on how to get things done more efficiently. They will also know when you're hard at work and that they probably shouldn't plan to do things with you during those times. Keeping them in the loop will make life easier for everyone. And let's face it, sometimes they're your taxi service getting you from Point A to Point B, so it's just considerate to let them in on where you are planning on going and when.

"I don't know the key to success, but the key to failure is trying to please everyone."
– Bill Cosby

If you want to be more detailed in your scheduling, make your own monthly calendar on a large piece of paper. To make easy changes to your timetable, you might consider buying a plastic-coated calendar with an erasable marker. Write down how much time each activity and chore requires. When you're thinking about the activities you're involved in, remember to add in the time it takes to get to and from practices, special events like tournaments, and time to rest. For example, you may be part of a swim club that meets every Sunday afternoon for an hour. Then you might have two or three weekend swim meets. Plus you have to rest – if you want to win a few races! Add to all this the half hour it takes to get to and from the pool each time you go. That adds up to a big portion of your schedule, and for only one activity!

There are other things that can take up your time besides chores and school. Don't forget to factor in family time and special events like birthdays, picnics, and vacations. Are your cousins coming in from out of town for a couple weeks this summer? You might want to spend some time with them instead of working nonstop. Then there are appointments with the dentist and the doctor. Everyone knows how long these things can take! If you're volunteering somewhere, don't give it up to make extra money. It's important to share your time, skills and energy with those who need it. Oh, and don't forget to set aside some strictly fun time. Use this time to relax, read, or hang out with your best buds.

Early Italian bankers used to conduct their business on street benches. The modern English word "bank" evolved from the word "banca" meaning bench.

59

MAY 12

8:00	walk Ms. Elliot's dog
8:45	school
9:00	
3:00	groceries for Mr. Field
3:15	
5:00	supper/ homework
5:15	
6:30	help Mr. Davis plant garden
6:30	
8:00	

MAY 13

8:00	deliver eggs
8:45	
9:00	school
3:00	
3:15	walk Mrs. Tibb's dog
4:15	Bank deposit MONEY!!
4:20	
4:30	
5:00	supper
5:30	

Another little trick that can help you better manage your time is to carry around a small date book. Let's say you're at school and your friend invites you to a birthday party at her house on the weekend.

You'll be able to check right away if you'll need to re-arrange your schedule to be a part of the special event. If you're free, you can jot it down in your date book right away. And add a note to remind you to let your parents know. Once you know you're free and your parents give you the OK, you can mark it on your main calendar. Don't forget to set aside time to make or buy your friend a gift!

TRUE STORY
Dynamo Duo!

CINDY NATIONS, 14, and LINDSAY NATIONS, 12, LOBCKHART, SOUTH CAROLINA

When Cindy and Lindsay need extra money to buy a new CD or the latest threads they don't ask mom and dad for the cash. "We brainstorm to try to come up with ideas of things we can do to earn the money," says Cindy.

These hard-working girls often team up for projects like yard sales. "We just go around the house, look for things we don't want anymore

like toys and clothes,"
says Cindy. Their mom also cleans out the house of unwanted things and splits her finds between the sisters. Cindy admits Lindsay has an easier time selling her stuff. At one yard sale Lindsay raked in $24 while Cindy took in just $8.

Sometimes the sisters work as part of group to achieve a larger goal. Last April, their church organized a trip to Myrtle Beach that would cost $80 per kid. To reduce the costs, they organized a car wash. It was hard work, but they managed to raise $500. That meant each kid paid only $20 to go on the trip.

Lindsay has also tried her hand in the service industry. One summer she looked after the neighbors' house while they were on vacation. She watered plants, fed the cats, and walked the dog. Total earnings: $10. She and a friend have also taken turns in being a companion to an elderly woman who had to stay in bed. For $2 a visit they would do chores and generally keep her company.

With all the money-making ideas this team has come up with, there's no chance these girls will ever be bored or broke!

So far, we've covered week-to-week or day-to-day scheduling. But many businesses have yearly cycles. Making a schedule will help you decide if you want and have the time to work all year round or just during the summer months. The *type* of work you choose to do will also have a big impact on whether you'll work part of the year or the entire year. Some jobs have periods when you can expect to be very busy and then have little to do the rest of the year. Others will keep you busy throughout the year. For example, if you're going to make Christmas ornaments, you might be moderately busy during the year taking orders and making ornaments. But come December, you'll probably be swamped. So it's OK to take some time off during the year and work extra long hours the two weeks before Christmas. Here are a couple questions you can ask yourself to help make a decision that is right for you:

ARE YOU WORKING TOWARDS A GOAL?

AIM HIGH: ASHANTI STARTED HER SINGING CAREER AT AGE 12 – AND WON HER FIRST GRAMMY NINE YEARS LATER.

Having a reason to earn a set amount of money can help you determine how long you'll have to work. Setting a clear goal also motivates you to do your job. You can have long-term or short-term goals. Try writing down your goals for your business. Is your goal to raise money for a charity? Are you trying to save for a summer trip? You can have more than one goal, too. Write down everything you want to accomplish through your work and then summarize it in one or two sentences.

One of the things this exercise will help you uncover is if you need to work all year or just a few months. If your goal is to raise lots of money to buy a new bike, it might take you all year. If you just want to collect as much money as you can to donate it to the local soup kitchen, then you'll probably only need to work during summer.

IS YOUR JOB SEASONAL?

Most outdoor work will be seasonal at some point. Take yard work. In spring, summer, and fall you can rake leaves, water gardens, paint decks, and plant flowers. In winter, you can shovel driveways. So if you live in an area with four distinct seasons, you will have to decide three things: Do you have the skills to work in each season? Do you have the time to work while going to school? Are you interested in working all year or would you rather take a few months off to relax and recharge?

Some jobs are not compatible with certain times of the year. You have to keep this in mind if you're planning to earn a set amount of money to buy a special item. If you plan to run an outdoor fresh fruit juice bar, you're pretty much limited to summer months. For one thing, juicy fresh fruit is hard to come by and expensive in the middle of winter. Second, you won't be able to operate an outdoor stand when it's chilly outside, not to mention that customer traffic will be nonexistent.

Seasonal can also refer to holidays. If you're into making and selling fudge, you can expect to be really busy around the Easter and Christmas holidays and less so throughout the year when you might only make fudge for an occasional birthday party.

Making a schedule when you're in business with a friend becomes a little more complicated. You have to consider not only your time and activities but also what your partner has on his or her plate. Have your friend make a schedule. Make sure all his or her activities, chores, and other time commitments are listed. Then bring your two schedules together and see if you can find time when both of you are available.

If coordinating a schedule that fits both your needs proves to be a struggle, it may be time to ask whether taking on a partner will help or hinder your work. Consider the following questions to discover if you'd be better off working in a team or going solo:

WHAT DO YOU HOPE TO ACHIEVE?

The key to working well with friends is getting along and having similar interests and goals. Of course, that doesn't mean you have to be good at the exact same things. In fact, it might be helpful to join forces with someone who can do things you don't know how to do very well. But the reason you're working together, and even working at all, should be similar. This is important because if, say, you're working to raise money to buy a new bike and your buddies are just working to buy a couple of CDs, you will want to work longer hours than your friends. Sooner or later this is going to cause friction. You will become frustrated at putting in so much more time than them. Your friends might feel like all you want to do is work, work, work, without having any fun. It's better to talk about what your goals are before setting up shop.

HOW WILL WORKING TOGETHER
AFFECT YOUR FRIENDSHIP?

How much do you get along with your friend?
Are you competitive with each other? A little
competition is great. It can push both of you to
do a better job. But if you're constantly com-
paring notes on who does a better job, you'll
end up fighting. No job is worth wrecking a
perfectly good friendship.

   And think about how much time you
already spend with your friend. Even best friends
need time away from each other. If you're already
on the same soccer team, swim team, and have
gone to camp together, explore the idea of
teaming up with another bud. Keep your best
friend for your time off. Besides, you might
gain another great friend by getting to know
him or her through work.

   What about going into business with your brother or sister?
You'll need to think about
how you get along when
doing chores around the
house. Do you easily
divvy up the work and
get it done quickly? Or
are you constantly bick-
ering about who's doing more?

Do you share a room with your sibling? Are you cool with that? If you feel that you get along well with your sis or bro, consider working together for extra cash. For one thing, you're already living in the same house, so you know where to find your partner if you have some business problems to work out.

IS PARTNERSHIP PRACTICAL?

Sometimes the type of work you're interested in doing is going to determine whether you work in a team or solo. Some jobs, like typing other students's papers and reports, are better done alone. But you can use a buddy or two if you're running a catering business. A helping hand in the kitchen is always a good idea. Even deliveries go faster when you're in two.

In other cases, it may just be impractical to team up with a friend. If your best bud lives across town, you might have a hard time getting together to make the hair clips you want to sell. If you have to ask your parents to drive you every day, there's a good chance you'll give up on your job before the summer is over.

If a partnership does turn out to be the best option, make sure to set the rules of the game. Talk about how you're going to deal with unexpected changes in schedules, how much notice you should give each other if you need to cancel, who works which holidays, and what happens if someone gets sick. Emergencies can happen to anyone, but if you constantly call up your friend at the last minute to tell him you won't be able to work that day, your business will be doomed – not to mention your friendship.

CHAPTER 6

Promoting Your Business

GETTING the word out that you're in business is an important part of your job. After all, how are people supposed to know what you can do for them if they've never heard of you? Think of your strategy in three steps. First, what are the important elements of good publicity? Second, what tools do you have, or are easy to make, to promote your business? Third, who should you target with your ads and how?

The easiest ways to promote your business are to make and distribute flyers and/or business cards. Before you rush out and print hundreds of flyers, think through what would make them attention grabbing. For instance, every business has a name and a **logo**. A logo is a symbol you use that will quickly remind people of you and your business. Think of what the golden arches do for McDonald's, or how the swoosh makes an automatic connection to Nike. The logo can have both a drawing and words. Try out a few different ideas and ask your parents and a close

friend which one they like best. Maybe they'll have suggestions on how to improve your idea.

The rest of the flyer or business card should be just as eye-catching. Flyers come in different shapes and colors. Colorful ads always get more attention than drab ones. But don't go overboard. Too many colors splashed all over the flyers can look too busy and just confuse people. Making so many color copies can also get expensive. Think of a theme that best suits what you're doing and decorate with that idea in mind. If you're a party planner, you might have a colorful border on your flyers and business cards with party hats and balloons. Starting a catering business? Dot your ads with a few chef hats, steaming soup bowls and cupcakes.

Flyers and business cards can be easily designed on your computer. Many programs have step-by-step instructions on how create a business card. *Check out some creative examples in this book and on our website at* **www.lobsterpress.com**. You can think up ideas that are more specialized for your business and print it out on pre-fitted business card paper, available at your local office supplies store. Flyers are just as easy. Print them out on regular size paper and

drop them in people's mailboxes or leave them on car windshields. Work your creativity and think of other ways to make your flyers stand out. What about making flyers that hang on doorknobs? Printing them on brightly colored paper?

But a good flyer or business card should be more than eye-catching. Getting all the key information about your business on your ads is the first step to good promotion.

There are five things every good flyer and business card should include: your name, your business' name and logo, your phone number and E-mail address, and a short description of the services you offer. If you're making flyers to announce a one-time yard sale or bake sale, remember to include dates, time, location and directions to your event. If you're making flyers for

FEELIN' THE HEAT?

Come visit

BILL & TED's CAR WASH / POPSICLE STOP

JULY 31st from 10:30am - 4:00pm

At the Thurston Community Center parking lot on High Street

All proceeds go to the Mertonville Mission

69

your ongoing business, include a run-down of the goods and/or services you offer, plus a list of your prices. Make sure that the font you use is clear and legible. You need potential clients to be able to understand the information that you are providing.

So where do you put them? You might be tempted to rush out and deliver as many flyers as you can as fast as you can. Well, that'll get the word out for sure. But you'll also be exhausted and your money and energy may have been spent for nothing. A better idea would be to think through where your flyers would have the biggest impact. The question is not *if* people will see them, but if the *right* people will see them. Think about it, if someone ten blocks away from your house asks you to mow their lawn, would you be able to get there with all your gear without asking mom and dad to drive you every week?

List the places where you think you could attract clients in your neigh-

QUIZ ZONE

Can You Talk Your Way Into Business?

Your ability to communicate with people in a clear way is an important business skill. Why? It will be key in getting customers. Whether you use flyers, business cards or a class presentation, if you know the ins and outs of your business and you're comfortable talking about it to anyone, you'll have an easier time selling your goods and services. Take this quiz to see how prepared you are to pitch your business. Then read up on how you can improve your sales ability.

On a scale of 1 to 5 (5 being excellent) how do you rate the following statements about yourself?

TURN TO THE END OF THE CHAPTER TO CHECK YOUR SCORE

1. I can talk about my product or service without relying on a prepared statement or notes.

score from 1 to 5

cont. on pg. 71

borhood. A few possibilities include: neighbors' houses up to two streets away from yours, where your parents work, your school bulletin board, community centers, grocery store bulletin boards, etc. Be sure to ask for permission before you post your ads in public places. Write down five places near you that you think will offer good visibility.

1. _____

2. _____

3. _____

4. _____

5. _____

If you have some money saved up, try buying a small ad in your local community paper. To get the best bang for your buck, buy a small ad in the local weekly paper rather than a large daily paper. You might want to ask your parents if they think the price is right, and to help you check if it is safe to give out information about yourself. If you're going hi-tech

QUIZ ZONE

2. I know which groups of people would be the best customers for my business; I know where to find them and how to reach them.

score from 1 to 5

3. My prices are fair because I've researched other businesses that provide similar products and/or services and I know how much they charge.

score from 1 to 5

4. I have clear, attention-grabbing flyers and business cards.

score from 1 to 5

5. I know what my competitors offer and I have a handful of reasons why my service is different and better.

score from 1 to 5

cont. on pg. 72

QUIZ ZONE

6. I practice my presentation so that I don't feel nervous when I talk about my business to people I hardly know.

score from 1 to 5

7. If people don't like my ideas, I respect their opinion and ask them how they would improve my ideas.

score from 1 to 5

8. I always follow up with clients who have already purchased from me. I like to know what they think of my product and if they would like to reorder.

score from 1 to 5

TURN TO PG. 73 TO CHECK YOUR SCORE

and placing an ad on the Internet, stick with sites that feature other community announcements. And again, get some ideas from your parents about what sites they think are safe and would work best for you.

You can also get a little wacky and creative in trying to reach your customers. And it doesn't have to be expensive, either. Some fun and easy ways to grab attention are: leaving a quick mention of your business at the end of your family voice-mail message, making and wearing a T-shirt with the name of your business on it, and speaking to your class about your business.

And don't underestimate your parents' ability to help, too. Ask your parents to put in a good word for you at their workplace and tell coworkers about what you do. If they find someone who is interested in what you do, you can take the next step in contacting your potential client.

QUIZ ZONE

Answers to Chapter 6 -
Can You Talk Your Way
Into Business?

If you scored...

SWEET TALKER: 30-40 POINTS

You're great at promoting your business. You are always well prepared to talk about what you do. You spend a lot of time thinking about your business and how to get new customers. Keep in mind, though, that you can overdo it. Not every casual conversation has to turn into a sales pitch. That can be annoying. So be careful about choosing the appropriate time to talk about your business.

TALKER IN TRAINING: 20-30 POINTS

You have all the basics down like making flashy flyers and snazzy business cards. But you're a little shy when it comes to talking to others about what you do, especially people you don't talk to very often. That's OK. There are a couple things you can do to make it easier. Write down on index cards three reasons why people should be interested in what you do or the products you sell. Then practice talking about them in front of your parents, sisters, brothers, and your best friend. Soon you'll feel confident enough to talk to just about anybody!

TONGUE-TIED: LESS THAN 20 POINTS

Promoting yourself is a real chore. Forget about talking about what you do, you're afraid of running into the neighbors when you're passing out your flyers. Don't give up. Ask a good friend to help you out. Maybe the two of you can pass out flyers together. If need be, your bud can help you explain your business to the people you meet. Ask your parents to pitch in. Perhaps they can take some of the flyers in to work. If any of their coworkers want to know more about what you do, you can prepare yourself with a few notes and call them on the phone. Eventually, it'll be no sweat to meet them face-to-face.

Chapter 7

Be A Pro!

SOMETIMES being a kid makes it hard for people to believe you can do your job properly. For whatever reason, some people may think you're too young, meaning that you'll be late or that you won't follow their instructions. This might seem like a form of discrimination, but it is up to you to prove them wrong! It won't be easy because you'll have to work twice as hard to convince them that not only are you responsible, but you're also the best kid on the block to get the job done right. It can be done! Here are some tips on how to show your clients that you're the one for the job. Once you prove yourself a professional, they'll keep coming back for more!

Being the best at what you do is the strongest incentive for people to hire you, but there are other things that can help make your case to adults. The way you behave and dress say a lot about your personality. You've probably heard the saying: You only have one chance to make a first impression. In most situations,

How Organized Are You?

Organization is a state of being. What that really means is if your room is a mess, chances are your business will be one too. Take this quiz to see if you need to add a little order to your life.

TURN TO THE END OF THE CHAPTER TO CHECK YOUR SCORE

1. You just crunched the last chip from a tasty bag of barbecue chips, but the kitchen garbage is full. You:

A. *leave it on the kitchen counter. Mom's going to pick up after you eventually.*

B. *take out the garbage.*

C. *squash the compact garbage until there's a tiny space to shove your bag in.*

cont. on pg. 78

it's true. Whether you're looking for work or already on the job always dress neatly. It doesn't matter if you're going to be mowing lawns all day, sweating and getting your hands dirty. If you know you're going be a mess, bring an extra T-shirt and change it midway through your jobs. Not only will you feel better, you won't look like you just ran a marathon!

If you're a babysitter, you know you're bound to get some gooey stuff on your shirt or pants when you feed Sweet Pea. Be prepared with a change of clothes. Bring along some sweatpants and an extra shirt. You don't want to have to explain to the parents of the kid how the mashed potatoes got all over you.

Another simple way to boost your credibility is to be polite. Just saying please and thank you can go a long way. Being polite also means taking into consideration that other people have a life of their own. If you're looking to drum up business and decide to go door to door asking neighbors if they need their lawns mowed, don't do it during dinnertime. You know how annoying it is when people try to sell you something over the phone when you're having dinner at home? Knocking at their door won't make you any more welcome!

Whether you call or show up on someone's doorstep, always start by asking if it's is a good time to talk. What's the point of launching into a two-minute pitch if the person has a pot of boiling water on the stove and doesn't hear a word you say? Be prepared to leave a flyer or business card if the person is too busy to talk to you. If someone you call doesn't have a few minutes to spare, ask when would be a good time to call back so you don't bug them by calling again and again when they're busy.

Sometimes you have to be a little creative when you're trying to make people believe that you can do the job right. If you're

2. Your friend calls you to say he wants you to return the video-game he lent you last week. You:

A. *say you'll be right over with the video-game and thank him for loaning it to you.*

B. *ask him to remind you again which videogame he lent you. You have tons of games lying all over your bedroom floor.*

C. *beg him to let you keep it a few more days. You have no idea where in the house it ended up – you might have to buy him a new one.*

3. It's Sunday afternoon and you're on your way to the movies with your friends. You've just had a peanut butter and jelly sand-wich. As you walk out the door, your kitchen counter looks like:

cont. on pg. 80

selling stationary and greeting cards, for example, it might be a good idea to give out a few free samples. Have a show-and-tell session at home with a handful of friends and give them a sample of your cards. When they take them home to their parents, they'll tell them they actu-ally saw you make them. Free samples are a great way to get your products out there, and your friends can give you a lot of help in marketing them.

And remember that scoring a job is no reason to stop showing your professionalism. Arrive for work on time and with all the tools you'll need. If you're mowing lawns and tending to gardens, don't assume all your neigh-bors have a weed whacker. Imagine what a disappointment it would be if your neighbors were planning an after-noon barbecue party and expected you to manicure their lawn in the morning only to see you show up at noon with-out a lawnmower. Make sure you know when you are expected and what you need to bring to get the job done.

If you're a babysitter, take with you some games, arts and crafts materials, or books. The kids might have all of these things at home. But if you have some new tricks in the bag, it will not only delight your little customer (making your job easier!) it will also impress her parents.

A responsible babysitter will also ask parents questions. Bring a contact list with you by making a copy of this one, or designing your own. You need to know where the parents can be reached, whom to call in case of emergency, bedtime and other special instructions they want you to follow. Many parents will leave this information on the fridge door but it's good to double check and ask if there's anything else they want done. Your interest in getting it just right will make them comfortable in leaving you with their children.

BABYSITTER'S CONTACT LIST

1. **Where the Parents will be:**
   Location:_____
   Phone number:_____
   Address:_____

2. **Emergency Contact Name and Number:**
   _____

3. **Time the Parents are expected home:**
   _____

4. **Child's bedtime:**
   _____

5. **Is the child taking any special medications?**
   Name of medication:_____
   Last given at:_____
   Next dose due at:_____
   Dosage:_____

6. **Any other special instructions:**
   _____
   _____

IN CASE OF EMERGENCY DIAL 9-1-1

Being a professional also means being organized. It is up to you to track your work so that all orders will be filled and paid for on time. From order forms to bills to receipts, the more organized you keep your materials, the more reliable and efficient you'll be.

One of the easiest ways to organize your paperwork is to set up folders to keep important business documents, letters, receipts

A. *a food fight just took place in your kitchen.*

B. *spotless and shiny.*

C. *You put the peanut butter back in the cupboard and the jelly in the fridge, but you left the dish and empty glass in the sink rather than put them in the dishwasher.*

4. How long does it take you to clean your room?

A. *15 minutes at the end of every day.*

B. *30 minutes – two or three times a week.*

C. *two hours every Saturday morning.*

5. When you rent a movie, the video store can expect to get it back:

a. *as soon as you've finished watching it, even if it's the same day you rented it.*

b. *a couple days later – which is usually a few days before it's actually due.*

c. *when you remember to bring it back – could be a month.*

TURN TO THE END OF THE CHAPTER ON PG. 83 TO CHECK YOUR SCORE

and bills at your fingertips. It doesn't have to be anything fancy. You can go to the dollar store and buy some filing folders and stash them in a box if you don't have a filing cabinet or a desk drawer.

Depending on the type of business you have you may need order forms. For example, if you sell homemade cookies, plant and flower seedlings, or stationary, order forms are a must. Take a look at the one opposite. There needs to be space on your order form to fill out the following information: customer's name, address, phone number, type of product they want, quantity, color, price, delivery date and time and any other special instructions. Check out the sample forms on our website and customize your own forms to suit your business. Once your clients place their order, this information is what you will need to make sure you get the job done properly. Don't forget to give the customer a copy, too.

When you return to your customers with completed orders, give them a bill. The bill, sometimes called an invoice, should include the delivery date, a detailed description of your work and how much it cost, the total amount they have to pay and the date by which they

Harriet's Homemade Hair Scrunchies
ORDER FORM
Customer Name: _____ Phone Number: _____
Address: _____
Type of Product: _____ Color: _____
Quantity: _____ Price: _____
Delivery/Pick-up date: _____
Special Instructions: _____

have to pay it. And of course, don't forget to say thank you! Again, make sure that you have your own copy of the bill; this is your proof that you have completed the job and are now expecting payment.

Be prepared to offer a receipt if they ask for one. It doesn't have to be anything fancy, take a look at the sample below. After payment, hand your customer this small slip of paper with the date, the items they purchased and the total amount that they paid you. Once you receive payment for your work, also mark "Paid" on your bill.

A good way to keep track of all this business is to develop a customer profile

---

NICK'S TULIP HOUSE

INVOICE

Customer Name: _____
Delivery Date: _____

Early Spring Mix......................$15.00

Planting service.......................$ 5.50

Extra compost.........................$ 5.50

Total..........$26.00

Payment Due: _____

Thank you!

Jill's Personalized Greeting Cards
For all your loved ones, on any occasion.

RECEIPT
Date: _____

Items purchased:
1 personalized................ $ 4.50
2 blank........................... $ 2.50 x 2
                    Total $ 9.50
                    Paid $10.00
                    Change $ 0.50

Thank you. Have a nice day!

database. All you need is a bunch of index cards and a small box – like a shoebox! When you've completed a job for a customer, make a card with his or her name on it along with a phone number, address, and date. Attach their old orders, bills and receipts so you know what business you did with them. Specify on their card if they had any special likes, dislikes or preferences, so you'll be reminded for the future. File these cards alphabetically. When you want to drum up more business you can call them back and ask them if they need to reorder or if they need your services again.

Chances are you're going to be doing most of your paperwork in your room. So to keep your room from turning into a zoo, set aside one corner as office space. Hang a bulletin board to keep urgent jobs in view. Make sure your schedule is in sight, too. If you have a desk, use it to neatly store paper clips, pens, stamps, a calculator, notepads, and customer files. If you don't have a desk in your room, simply get a storage box and keep your work items all together.

In the end, however, you have to accept that in some cases you just can't convince others that you're the right person for the job. It's good to be persistent, but don't push so hard that you become annoying. Some adults, for whatever reason, don't want to hire kids. If you've tried a few times with certain people and they won't even listen to you, it's better to cut your losses and move on. After all, you don't want to waste all your time convincing one person when there may be dozens of others willing to hire you!

QUIZ ZONE

Answers to Chapter 7 -
How Organized Are You?

Score Your Answers...

1. A = 0; B = 2; C = 1
2. A = 2; B = 1; C = 0
3. A = 0; B = 2; C = 1
4. A = 2; B = 1; C = 0
5. A = 1; B = 2; C = 0

MESSING WITH SUCCESS: 0-3 POINTS

There's no way you'll be able to run a business properly if your personal life is any indication of your organizational skills. It's time to start putting things in order. Sometimes all you need to keep the clutter from taking over is a place to put all your stuff. Make sure you have enough storage space in your room. All it takes is 10 to 15 minutes to tidy up every day to keep things in control.

CLUTTER LOVER: 4-6 POINTS

Not bad, but not great either. You can go either way – you may be on the brink and slip off the wagon any day if you don't put in some extra time cleaning up. Don't give up. In fact, get excited about not only cleaning things up but also trying out new ideas that will motivate you to get organized. Check out the tons of cool containers and boxes that can make it easy to clear clutter.

NEAT FREAK: 7-10 POINTS

You've got everything under control. Your room looks like a picture out of a trendy home furnishings catalog. It's going to be easy for you to keep all of your work papers in order. But don't go overboard. It's not worth spending hours making everything perfect and spotless when you could be using some of that time actually getting more work done.

CHAPTER 8
How Much Money Do You Need?

ALL of the thinking you've done up to now will help you write a great **business plan**. A business plan is like a guidebook. It will help you find the best way to success. It contains your goals, how you plan to achieve them and what resources you will need to make it happen. Notice that each of these steps will probably require you to think about money – how to raise it, save it, and spend it.

Start by writing down what you want your business to achieve. This is your **mission statement**. Why did you start this business? It could be because you want to buy yourself a game console, a new outfit, a guitar, go on a trip, help others, even save the world! Summarize your goal in one or two sentences and write it down.

Next, think about the market research you did earlier to figure out who else was doing what you want to do.

TRUE STORY

DANIEL MILLER JR., 15, PITTSBURGH, PENNSYLVANIA

Daniel's been running **Daniel Miller Jr. Custom Postcards** out of his house since he was 9 years old. A computer whiz, Daniel uses his desktop publishing skills to create thousands of postcards, letterheads, flyers, invitations, and even funeral programs!

His first sale – the result of a postcard to a favorite teacher – may have been a coincidence, but hard work has kept his business going strong despite early obstacles. "At first, many adults didn't believe I was doing the work on my own," says Daniel. "They thought my mom was making the cards." So to prove his passion and talent, he would book free space at the local library to promote his work. "People were fascinated about how much I knew about my business."

cont. on pg. 88

You also looked at who would be interested in your goods and services. If there were others, including professionals, who were offering your products or services, you also got an idea of how much they were charging. Write all this information down in your business plan under the heading "Market Analysis and Data."

Remember when you came up with ideas to promote your business? Well now you can write it down in your business plan so you can refer to it again and again when you need to boost your client roster. Use the heading "Promotion and Advertising."

This is also where you have to start thinking about how much it will cost to get your business off the ground. Though there are some promotional tactics that don't cost a penny – such as word-of-mouth advertising through classmates or referrals by current clients – other promotional tools do require a little cash.

Make a list of all the advertising ideas you came up with earlier. Then figure out what tools you will need to make them happen. Whatever items you already have at home can be crossed off your list. Whatever is left is what you'll need to buy. For example, let's say you've chosen to advertise yourself as a math tutor by posting flyers at your church and community center bulletin boards, handing out business cards to the parents of neighborhood kids younger than yourself and letting classmates and teachers know of your availability.

Your list would look like this:

Flyers..............**$5.00**
(1 pack of printer paper)
Business cards.....**$10.00**
(1 pack of printable business)
Word-of-mouth......**$0.00**

Your promotion and advertising expenses therefore come to $15.00. Can you improve on this price? Think of bargain places where you can get your stuff for cheap. Promotional materials,

INTERNET INSIGHT
www.csuchico.edu/sife

Wise Kid, Wealthy Kid Youth Entrepreneurship Camp:

HELD AT THE CALIFORNIA STATE UNIVERSITY, CHICO CAMPUS. FIFTH AND SIXTH GRADERS WRITE BUSINESS PLANS AND RECEIVE $25 SEED MONEY, THEN SET UP SHOP AT A CARNIVAL.

as well as stuff to stock your home office, can be found at dollar stores.

In addition to office and promotion expenses that come up every once in awhile, some expenses require you to spend only once or twice a year. If you decide to take a sewing class or sign up for a wood-working workshop, that's a one-time expense.

Estimate how much each type of expenses will cost and write the total down in your business plan under the heading "Expenses." You may have to tap into your savings for start-up expenses like supplies. If you don't have any money saved up, you can ask your parents for a small loan. But make sure to pay them back as soon as you start making some money. Explain your goals to your parents by showing them your business plan and arranging a loan agreement *A loan agreement, like the one on our website at* **www.lobsterpress.com**, will make clear how much money you want to bor-row and when you plan to pay them back.

Community programs have also helped to improve Daniel's business skills. One of the first ones was a summer camp he attended when he was 9 years old. At the National Foundation for Teaching Entrepreneurship he learned to write a business plan and read many books on how to run a successful business.

His goal is not only to run a successful business but also to use it to earn enough money to fund cancer research. Daniel is determined to one day have his own research center to help find cures for all types of cancer – he's already teamed up with cancer researchers at Carnegie Mellon University! His goal hit close to home when his grandfather died of cancer in 1998.

Advice for other kids who are interested in becoming entrepreneurs? "I tell them they can run a business as well, and that it's not just for adults," Daniel said. "The important thing is to have a goal in mind – to have a dream."

The information that you have in your business plan will now help you calculate a good price for your goods and services. Setting prices can be tricky, but if you think it through carefully, you can come up with a fair price that will attract enough customers and keep you in business.

Let's say you've decided to be an entertainer at kids' parties. Start off by deciding how much money you want to make and by when you want to make it. Say you want to make $500 in 6 months. Now list the expenses you'll have to do your job. As a party entertainer you'll need a clown suit, balloons, toys for games, signs, posters, order forms, an appointment book, and extra stuff that's bound to pop up.

Your list will look like this:

EXPENSES

ITEMS	COST
Clown suit	$25.00
Balloons	$ 5.00
Toys for games	$10.00
Signs, posters, order forms	$ 5.00
Appointment book	$ 2.00
Extras	$ 5.00

Your total expenses will be $52. So you have to earn $552 to make the $500 you set as a goal and to pay off $52 of expenses. How much do you want to charge for each party? You figure $20 is fair. Let's see if that's realistic:

If you divide $552 by 6 months, you get $92 – the amount you have to earn each month to reach your goal. If you charge $20 per party, you'll have to book roughly one party a week to make $500 in 6 months. That might be realistic in summertime, but it might be difficult to work that hard during school time. So you might have to either charge a little more per party or work a few extra months to meet your goal of $500.

Part III
MANAGING YOUR MONEY

CHAPTER 9
Four-Jar Method

HALF of all businesses go out of business in their first year, usually because of poor planning or lack of market research. The previous chapters should help you avoid those obstacles, but another important way to ensure your business succeeds is to become a smart money manager. At the end of every month, you should grab your ledger – this is the book that you keep track of your spending with – and put your accounts in order. Tally up all the money you made (also called the *gross profit*), subtract all your expenses, and the total you come up with is your net profit. During the month, make sure you save the receipts for everything you buy. They will help you keep track of your spending in case you forget to jot down an expense in your ledger. Once you're sure of how much money is left over, you can start thinking about what you want to do with it. With careful management, you'll be able to use some of the money to buy things you need and want right away as well as save some for future use.

The simplest way to keep track of your money is to get four jars (shoeboxes work just fine, too) and label them as follows: Savings, Spending, Investing, and Charity. Ideally, you would put about 10% of your net profit in Savings, 10% in Investing, 10% into your Charity jar, and the remaining 70% into the Spending jar.

The amount of money you put into each jar can vary a little depending on your long-term and short-term goals. Your spending jar has the bulk of your earnings because it will cover the money you spend to run your business as well as short-term goals like buying CDs, clothes, and other things you might need day to day. But you will also need to think about how much money you need to save to achieve long term goals such as taking a summer camp trip or buying a new digital camera. While these goals are more expensive, you usually have more time to achieve them. There's nothing stopping you from juggling the percentages of profit that will go into each jar according to the goals you have set.

SAVING

Your saving jar stores money that you will eventually take to the bank for safekeeping. If you don't already have a bank account, you'll be able to open one with your savings. In return for keeping your money at a bank, you'll earn interest, which is usually a small percentage of the money you have in your account. You'll be allowed to withdraw and deposit money from your savings account whenever you want.

INVESTING

Putting money in your investing jar is another way to plan for your future, whether it's next week, next summer, or next year. Sometimes saving your money in a bank account won't make your money "grow" because the interest you earn from a bank isn't enough to cover large expenses. You may want to consider investing in stocks (where you are essentially buying a part of a company) and mutual funds (which groups the stocks of several companies). If you choose wisely, these investments will make your money grow much faster than if you simply socked your cash in a jar or bank account.

INTERNET INSIGHT

www.ncee.net

National Council on Economic Education:

A GREAT, COLORFUL SITE WITH TONS OF FUN ACTIVITIES THAT WILL SHARPEN YOUR FINANCIAL SKILLS.

CHARITY

Setting aside 10% in your charity jar is another way, besides volunteering, that you can give back to your community. You may not be giving out million-dollar checks and your donations may not make the front page of the local paper, but your contribution is still helping someone in need. Every little bit counts when it comes to helping others who are less fortunate than you are; the goal is to make your community the best place to live.

SPENDING

The spending jar is for stuff you want or need for yourself. Seventy percent is a large chunk, but a lot depends on this pot. From clothes to entertainment to birthday gifts, your spending money will have to take you a long way. This jar will also feed your work expenses, but remember to keep track of what it costs to run your business by listing work-related purchases in your ledger under "expenses". It's important to know how much you spend keeping your business afloat because that figure will help determine if you're charging the right amount for your work. If you're constantly dipping into your personal cash to cover for business-related expenses, you're probably not getting paid enough for your goods and services.

"Success is getting what you want. Happiness is wanting what you get."
– Dale Carnegie

CHAPTER 10

Saving: From Piggy Banks to Bank Accounts

PUTTING your money in a bank account makes sense for several reasons. First of all, it's safer than keeping it in your piggy bank or under the mattress! Second, you'll be able to earn a little extra money in interest just by keeping it in an account. Third, you'll develop the healthy habit of saving. And finally, you'll be able to take advantage of other financial services a bank has to offer, which could come in handy for a small business owner like yourself.

To open any kind of account at the bank you'll need a social security number (SSN) or a social insurance number (SIN). What is an SSN or SIN? And where do you get it? An SSN, as it is called in the U.S., and an SIN, as it is called in Canada, is a government-issued number that identifies you. Many people get one as soon as they are born. Others get it when they have to open up a bank account and get a job. Ask your parents if you already have one. If you don't, go to the bank or post office and ask for an application, fill it out and send it to the federal government. Once you receive a number, you'll be able to open a bank account. An exception may be made to this rule if you qualify for a children's account at your bank. In this case, all you may need is a birth certificate. Check with your local branch for more details.

One of the first things you will do when opening your bank account is complete a signature card. That's a piece of paper with your signature on it that the bank keeps in its files. So when you go to the bank to deposit or withdraw money, the bank can check to see that the signature on the deposit or withdrawal slip matches the one on the signature card. That way the bank can be sure that you are the holder of the account. You will also be asked to choose a PIN, which stands for Personal Identification Number. This is another way the bank can help keep your money secure. You will be asked to provide the number when you withdraw or transfer money, so memorize it and keep it in a safe place (but not in your wallet or near your bank card).

QUIZ ZONE

What Kind of Spender Are You?

What comes in must go out – at least some of it. If you save money, chances are you're going to spend it. Take this quiz to get an idea of how you spend your money and pick up some tips on how to improve your spending choices.

TURN TO THE END OF THE CHAPTER TO CHECK YOUR ANSWERS

1. When I get cash gifts for my birthday, I:

A. *Already know what I'm going to buy with it; the money is practically spent before I can put it in my pocket.*

B. *Add it all to my savings jar; spending is a bad thing unless you absolutely need something.*

C. *Spend some of the money on myself – it is my birthday after all – and save the rest.*

cont. on pg. 99

98

QUIZ ZONE

2. When I want something that costs more money than I have, I:

A. Beg mom and dad to give me the money.

B. Do extra chores around the house to earn more money and keep saving until I have enough to buy the item.

C. Borrow money from my friend, Moneybags.

3. If I get a poor grade on a test, I:

A. Go to the mall and spend all my money buying things to make me feel better.

B. Go to my room, shut the door, and study all night.

C. Go home, study for an extra half hour, and then join friends for a milkshake.

cont. on
pg. 100

If you're going to be using the bank to store your money, you should get to know who's who at the branch where you do business. There are often dozens of people working at a bank, but you only really need to know three key figures: the teller, cashier, and bank manager. The teller is the person at the counter that helps you do your transactions. The cashier is the person, usually inside a secure, glass-paneled cubicle at the center of the bank, working to physically get you the cash you requested or storing the cash you want to deposit. The teller hands the cashier the cash you want to deposit and gets from the cashier the money you want to take out. The bank manager is in charge of the employees at the bank and making sure customers are well served. You can ask to make an appointment to talk to the manager. But why would you? Well, at some point you'll want to use other services and the manager can help you figure out who is the best person at the bank to answer your questions.

SAVINGS ACCOUNTS

There are two types of simple savings accounts: a passbook and a statement account.

99

QUIZ ZONE

4. If I suddenly inherited $1 million, I would:

A. *Spend some money to celebrate my good fortune with family and friends and find ways to make the rest of the money grow.*

B. *Never again worry about working and saving money. I would just spend, spend, spend!*

C. *Sock away all the money. I'm going to be the richest kid ever!*

4. When I want to buy family and friends gifts, I:

A. *Buy things when they're on sale and make some of the gifts myself – like bookmarks, personalized dog food dishes, etc.*

B. *I don't give gifts. They're too expensive and I'm a kid. I'm not expected to give gifts, am I?*

C. *At the last minute, buy every gift and spend nearly all my money.*

TURN TO THE END OF THE CHAPTER ON PG. 105 TO CHECK YOUR ANSWERS

If you request a passbook, you'll have a small booklet that keeps track of the money you deposit and withdraw from the account. You'll take the passbook with you when you go to the bank and the teller will electronically update all the activity on the account. Your book will show all the transactions with dates and interest you earned. In a statement account, your transactions and interest will appear on a printed record, which is mailed to you every month or at the end of every quarter (every three months).

Each time you take money to the bank, you'll fill out a deposit slip. That's a piece of paper you'll give with your cash to the teller. You can get these slips at the bank, usually in one of the cubbyholes on the desk beside you where you're standing in line. You'll fill in the date and the amount of money you're depositing. There's also a slot to write in any amount you wish to withdraw at the same time. Then sign it and hand it to the teller, who will verify the form to make sure the math adds up, give you the money you requested, and update your account balance. You may also go to the bank and simply need to withdraw money. In this case, you fill out a withdrawal form for the amount you want.

You can also withdraw and deposit money without the hassles of waiting in line by using an ATM (Automatic Teller Machine). Just slip your bankcard into the slot and follow the directions that come up on the screen. But be careful about fees; if you use an ATM that is not from the bank with which you do business, you'll be charged extra for the service.

OTHER ACCOUNT OPTIONS

Once your business picks up speed and you start stashing away larger amounts of cash, there are other types of savings accounts that you can eventually pour money into. A teller or a bank manager can help you make the right choices for you. A money market account, for example, gives you a little more interest and lets you write a certain number of checks each month. The one drawback is that you have to keep a certain amount of money in the account at all times to avoid paying fees.

INTERNET INSIGHT

www.saveforamerica.org

THE NAME
SAYS IT ALL.
TAKE A LOOK
AT SOME GREAT
ADVICE ON HOW
TO SAVE.

COOL BONUS:
SOME OF YOU
GET TO OPEN
AND MANAGE
A BANK ACCOUNT
ONLINE!

If you want to earn even more interest on your money, you can place your cash in a certificate of deposit or a term deposit. Here's how it works: You give the bank your money, and the bank gives you a document that says it promises to repay you the money plus a certain percentage (usually a couple of percentage points more than you would get by leaving your money in a savings account). There are some rules you have to follow to get this deal. You usually need a minimum amount of about $1,000 to buy a certificate and you can't take out the money for a fixed amount of time. It could be six months, a year, 18 months or even three years – whatever you agree to. The longer you keep it in, the higher the interest rate you earn. If you take out the money before the period you agreed to keep it in the account, you pay a penalty.

INTEREST

So how does interest work, anyway? Why does the bank pay you interest on savings accounts? Basically, the bank is paying you to use your money. The bank is a business and one of the services it offers is lending money. It lends money to people who need to buy houses, cars and other personal items as well as to other businesses that need cash to run their business. When banks lend money, they charge interest. For example, they might lend your parents $5,000 to buy a car. Your parents will owe the bank $5,000 plus, say, 6% interest. Six percent of $5000 is $300, so in total your parents will owe $5,300. The interest banks pay to customers for using their money is lower than the interest they get from borrowers. That's one way banks make money and stay in business!

You can earn interest in two ways: simple and compound. Simple interest means interest is calculated only on the original amount you put in. For example, if you have $200 in your savings account and you're earning 3% interest, you'll get $6. The next time interest is paid out? You'll also get $6. But if your account lets you earn compound interest, you'll be earning 3% of $206 the next time interest is paid, which is $6.18. Now that doesn't seem like a big deal, but it will add up to big bucks in the long run because the base amount grows even if you don't put in extra money. Don't worry – banks use compound interest with savings

INTERNET INSIGHT

www.practical moneyskills.com

OK, EVEN THOUGH THIS SITE IS SPONSORED BY VISA, IT HAS A BUNCH OF GAMES, TIPS AND OTHER ACTIVITIES TO HELP YOU LEARN ABOUT BUDGETING, SAVING AND INVESTING.

accounts, though they may calculate it on a quarterly basis (every three months). Some savings bonds (certificates you get from the government when you lend it money) offer simple interest.

CHECKS AND DEBITS

Most kids don't get a checking account until they go away to college or they get a full-time job. A checking account lets you write checks to withdraw money from your account. Face it, right now you're not really going to need access to large amounts of cash, pronto! At the most, you may find a debit card useful. A debit card looks like a credit card, but is really just plastic that lets you access cash in your savings account. You can use them at ATMs and where merchants accept them. There are limits to how much you can withdraw from your account with a debit card. And that's a good thing, because it can be easy to overspend when you don't actually part with the bills!

QUIZ ZONE

Answers to Chapter 10 -
What Kind of Spender Are You?

Score Your Answers...

1. A = 0; B = 1; C = 2
2. A = 0; B = 2; C = 1
3. A = 0; B = 1; C = 2
4. A = 2; B = 0; C = 1
5. A = 2; B = 1; C = 0

IF YOUR SCORE IS 0-3 POINTS

You're a big spender! The good news is that you should have all the things you want by now. The bad news is that you're probably broke. Spending is not a bad thing. But you should also think about saving for long-term goals that can cost a little more than the stuff you buy every week, like a concert or an afternoon at the amusement park. It also wouldn't be a bad idea to simply save money so that it grows.

IF YOUR SCORE IS 4-7 POINTS

You understand the value of the dollar. You work hard to earn it and you don't like to spend it. But what good is money if you can't enjoy it a little? Every now and then it's important to reward yourself for working so hard. Share your good fortune with others, too. No one expects you to buy big, expensive gifts for birthdays, Christmas or Bar Mitzvahs. But if you spend a little money on a small gift and make a greeting card, you'll feel great about making someone else feel extra special on an important day.

IF YOUR SCORE IS 8-10 POINTS

You have it all figured out! You're a great spender and strike a good balance between saving and spending money. You don't spend money to feel better when you have the blues (that's called emotional spending, by the way). And you shop around for bargains. Look around and see if you can help a friend with their spending choices. Offer some of the tips you use to make wise spending and saving decisions.

CHAPTER 11

Spending: Cha-ching! It's Mine!

BEFORE you even spend a dime, you should learn to distinguish between needs and wants. It might seem pretty basic. But you can get them confused more often than you think. How many times have you told your parents you NEED a new pair of jeans when you had a closet full of clothes? What you meant to say was that you really WANTED a new pair of jeans. The word "need" adds a sense of urgency that you hope your parents will cave to. The same thing happens when you're out shopping on your own. If that little voice in your head uses the word need instead of want, you'll end up buying lots of stuff you really shouldn't.

Of course, it's OK to occasionally buy something because you want it, as long as you understand that your survival doesn't depend on it. If you want a certain item but know you can do without it, you'll be more likely to consider the price. Maybe right now is not the right time to buy it since it's too expensive. You might hold off until it goes on sale, or you might shop around for a better price. Delaying gratification, or putting off buying something you want until the price is in line with what you're willing to spend, will stop you from overspending. You might even reconsider buying the item at all.

Overspending, or confusing what you want and need, doesn't just happen when you're buying personal items.

As a small-business owner, you'll be tempted to buy lots of gadgets that you think will make your business better. Fancy calculators, funky pens, leather-bound date books — all these things are great if you want to look good. But they're not necessary for you to run a successful business. In fact, they actually might eat up a large chunk of your profits. Better to be frugal and successful, than to look good and be broke. Besides, take heart in knowing that most successful adult businesspeople are not big spenders at all. In fact, they're quite frugal. Need proof? Of the more than 7 million millionaires in the world, 80% of them drive second-hand cars!

CURB YOUR SHOPPING

Setting goals is a sure-bet way to manage your spending. Use both short-term and long-term goals to guide your shopping and buying decisions. Say your short-term goal is to start your own business so you can have extra cash to buy CDs. To make sure you have the money to buy the CDs you want, you have to avoid spending a buck here and a buck there on everyday items like snacks or gadgets. It may only seem like you're spending a small, insignificant amount, but it's actually chipping away at the $20 you'll need to buy one or two CDs you really want.

THE TRADING OF BUCKSKIN FURS IN COLONIAL TIMES CREATED THE NAME "BUCK" FOR DOLLAR.

Long-term goals make you even more disciplined in your spending because they usually require a larger amount of cash. Let's say you want to save money to be able to take a school band trip to Europe next year. Saving a couple of dollars each month isn't going to get you to your destination. You're going to have to be serious about cutting your spending and shopping wisely to get the best deals on the things you do buy.

There are four key ways to make sure you're spending wisely. The first two are simple. First, always use a list when you're out shopping for several things. Having a focus will stop you from just grabbing stuff because you think you might need it. Second, avoid last-minute shopping like the plague! How many times have you spent a small fortune on a frivolous gift for someone because you went shopping on Christmas Eve?

The next tips require more time and planning. You can do two things to make sure you're getting the best deal. Always compare prices between different stores. If you need to buy a new scanner for your desktop publishing business, check out all the major office supply stores before you buy. Find out if there are sales coming up. It might be worth waiting a couple days if you don't have an urgent project. And you don't have to buy brand new all the time. Check out the local paper to see if there's a used scanner you can get your hands on. Ask friends if they know anyone who might have a scanner they don't use and are willing to sell.

The other way is to learn to calculate the value of what you're buying. Buying bulk isn't always cheaper. And a lower price doesn't necessarily mean you're getting a good deal. Calculate the price you're paying per unit. What does that mean? If you see two packages of white bond printer paper and one costs $10 and the other $12, don't automatically grab the $10 pack. It might have slightly fewer sheets even if the package seems to be the same size. Look closely to the number of sheets in each package. Divide the price by the number of sheets and you have the price per unit. Luckily, you don't have to shop around with a calculator since many stores now do the math for you and put it in small print on the price tag on the shelf.

A FEW WORDS ON CREDIT CARDS...

Credit

You may be too young to whip out a credit card and yell, "Charge it!" but it's never too early to know how credit cards work. Credit card companies offer to pay for what you buy with your promise to pay them back. Every month they will send you a

IN ROMAN
TIMES,
SOLDIERS
WERE OFTEN
PAID WITH
SALT.
OUR WORD
"SALARY"
COMES FROM
THE LATIN
WORD FOR
SALT,
"SALARIUM."

monthly bill listing all the items you bought, when you bought them, how much you spent, and when your payment is due. If you don't pay the full amount each month, you'll be charged interest. And if you're late with your payment, you'll be charged a fee. Major credit card companies like Visa, MasterCard, Discover, and American Express let you buy goods and services at any business that accepts their cards.

Like cash, credit cards should be handled with care. It's much safer to use a credit card when you're buying big-ticket items rather than carrying around a big wad of cash. And they can come in handy in an emergency when you don't have cash in your pocket. For example, when you're old enough to drive, you might have a credit card in case you run out of gas or your car breaks down and you need to pay for a towing.

But keep in mind that it's also really easy to get in over your head with debt when you're spending with a credit card. Since you don't actually need to have as much cash as the card lets you spend, you can get into trouble. In any case, developing good spending habits now will go a long way in making sure you know how to use credit cards responsibly.

CHAPTER 12

Investing: The Stock Market

IF you're looking for a way to make your money grow to achieve a long-term goal, like saving for college, consider investing in the stock market. Before you start investing, get to know what the stock market is all about and how it works. Learning about investing will help you decide if you have the personality to play the game. The stock market can be a great place to earn big bucks, but you can also risk losing your shirt! But don't worry, if you do your homework, with lots of research, learning and persistence, you can be reasonably sure to make money in the long run.

Let's start with what is sold at this market: stock. Stock is a share in a business. When you buy a share, you buy a part in the company. You, along with everyone else who bought shares in

that company, are a shareholder. You're entitled to know what businesses the company is involved in, how much money it's spending and how much money it's making, as well as what it intends to do with the money in the future. When turning a profit, some companies pay a percentage of profit to shareholders. These pay-outs are called dividends. Of course, it's your responsibility to read and understand all this information. Companies send out annual reports to all shareholders to show the earnings, sales, expenses and profits of every quarter. The reports make for some heavy reading, but ask an adult to help you understand the most important parts. And you don't have to wait for the annual

QUIZ ZONE ?

Are You A Smart Investor?

One way to make your money grow is to invest it. Do you know where your money goes when you buy stocks? Are you aware of how much risk is involved in any given investment? Test your knowledge by taking this quiz.

TURN TO THE END OF THE CHAPTER TO CHECK YOUR SCORE

1. If you buy a company's stock:

A. *You have lent your money to the company.*

B. *You are paying the company's expenses.*

C. *You own a part of the company.*

cont. on pg. 116

report to come out to know what's going on. Read the business section in your newspaper regularly and check out the financial sections of news websites for up-to-the-minute news about companies.

So where do stocks come from? When a company needs money to expand its business, it goes public. Going public means the company will sell a certain amount of shares at a certain price to the investment bank. The first time shares of a company are sold is called an initial public offering. Having bought all the stock, investment bankers or brokers will then sell it to the public. The buying and selling of shares is the investment bank's or broker's business; when you buy and sell your shares, the investment bank makes a cut from the exchange.

Stocks are traded, meaning bought and sold, on exchanges. The major ones in North America include the New York Stock Exchange (NYSE), the American Stock Exchange (AMEX), the Toronto Stock Exchange (TSE) and the Montreal Stock Exchange. The National Association of Securities Dealers Automatic Quotation System (NASDAQ) sells stocks not listed with an exchange. There are also several other major exchanges around the world such as the German Stock Exchange, the Tokyo Stock Exchange and the London Stock Exchange.

The best way to look for companies to invest in is to think about what you know and like. By investing in companies that make products you're interested in, you're more likely to understand how they do business and what chances they have of being successful in the long run. Your interest will motivate you to research the company so that you know where you're putting your money. Other ways you can find good companies to invest in is to ask a financial advisor for leads or ask your parents to help you sort through some of the more successful picks they may have made. As a first-time investor, you want to get as much information as possible from research and talking to experts so that you make the best possible decisions with your hard-earned money.

OK, let's work through a real example so that all this makes more sense. Say you're a Spider-Man fan. Do a little research and you'll find out that the company that owns Spider-Man comics,

QUIZ ZONE

2. If you buy stock of a new company:

A. *You're sure to make money because they have new products to sell.*

B. *You can lose all the money you invested.*

C. *You lose only half the money you invested.*

3. Emily owns a wide variety of stocks, bonds, and mutual funds to reduce the risk of losing money. Her strategy is called:

A. *Saving*

B. *Diversifying*

C. *Spending*

cont. on pg. 117

movies, and merchandise is called Marvel Enterprises. Marvel is a publicly traded company. If you wanted to buy one of its shares today, you'll have to pay $25, plus a transaction fee to a brokerage firm (which can be as low as $15 if you do it online or as much as $100).

So now you own one share of Marvel. If you hold on to it and the share price goes up, you'd make money when you sell it. But if you sell it when the share prices goes below what you bought it for, you'd lose money. There's no guarantee when it comes to stock prices. There are many things that can affect stock prices: the overall health of the economy and performance of the company itself are two major indicators. Supply and demand also comes into play. If there are more people who want to buy the stock than there are sellers, the price of a stock will go up. If the economy is doing badly and the company reports terrible earnings, there will be more sellers than buyers, so the price will go down.

The best way to play the stock market game is to start out with play money.

QUIZ ZONE

4. Connor wants to take some of his savings and invest in a mutual fund. This is a good idea because:

A. *Mutual funds always earn more than savings accounts.*

B. *Mutual funds are managed by experts at picking investments.*

C. *Mutual funds are risk free.*

5. Over the past several decades, the type of investment that has made money grow the most for investors has been:

A. *Stocks*

B. *Savings accounts*

C. *Keeping it under your mattress*

TURN TO THE END OF THE CHAPTER ON PG. 121 TO CHECK YOUR SCORE

Internet Insight

www.youngmoney.com

YOUNG MONEY MAGAZINE OFFERS A FANTASY STOCK MARKET GAME FOR BEGINNING INVESTORS. YOU GET $100,000 PLAY MONEY, AND THE TOP PLAYERS GET A FREE SUBSCRIPTION TO THE MAGAZINE.

Pretend you have $500 to invest. Think of your favorite things: computer games, CDs, movies. Are the companies that make those things publicly traded? Take the PlayStation game console. Sony, a publicly traded company, makes it. Grab a newspaper like the Wall Street Journal, Investor's Business Daily, or The Globe and Mail – even the business section of a major city daily paper will do. When you hit the pages with a sea of tiny numbers and letters, don't be horrified – you're at the right place. What you're looking at are company names and a bunch of data about their performance. Some newspapers even include company ticker symbols. For example, Marvel's ticker symbol is MVL and Sony's SNE. Look for Sony in the NYSE columns. Stocks are listed alphabetically.

Now let's go through some of the important information you can glean from the numbers beside the company name. "Yld" stands for yield – yield is like interest, a percentage of what you have invested, or loaned to, the company. This is the cash you can expect to get from your investment in this stock. "Div" represents the approximate amount of dividend per share to be paid annually. "PE" stands for price-to-earnings ratio. It compares the current price of one share vs. the annual earnings per share of the company. So if you divide the current price of the share by the earnings per share, you'll get the PE ratio. An average PE hovers around 15. "Vol 100s" tells you how many shares of that stock exchanged hands that day. Multiply the number you see by 100 (a round lot of shares; an odd lot is less than 100 shares) and that's the total number. "Hi" is the highest price that shares were exchanged that day, while "Lo" is the lowest. "Close" refers to the price of the share in the last trade of the day. "Net Chg" tells you the difference between the day's close vs. the day before. If the price went down, you'll see a minus sign before the number; if it went up, you'll see a plus sign.

Now take the close price and see how many Sony shares you can buy with your fantasy $500. Check back every day for a couple months to see if you're making money or losing. You can choose to buy stocks in more than one company. In fact, many investors do just that to diversify their portfolio. That just means they don't want to put all their eggs in the same basket. Your investment portfolio can include stocks, bonds, and other securities. Having more than one stock means that your future

Internet Insight

www.smg2oo.org

HERE YOU ALSO GET A FANTASY $100,000 TO INVEST. IT'S A GAME, BUT YOU'LL BE LEARNING FINANCIAL AND ECONOMIC CONCEPTS THAT WILL BE KEY TO YOUR FUTURE WHETHER OR NOT YOU DECIDE TO RUN A BUSINESS.

doesn't depend completely on the success of one company. If one stock performs poorly but two others do very well, you're still making money.

There are other shares you can buy besides those offered on behalf of individual companies. Mutual funds are one example. A mutual fund is a group of investors pooling their money to buy a group of stocks, bonds, and other securities. This type of investment is perfect if you don't have the time to follow individual stocks yourself. A fund manager controls the mutual fund. A fund manager uses knowledge, experience, and research to choose the company stocks that will be included in the fund. You can find information on mutual funds in the same papers mentioned above, but there are also specialized publications like the weekly Morningstar Mutual Funds and the monthly Kiplinger Mutual Funds.

Don't be overwhelmed by all this stock market data. Read it one company at a time. Start with the ones that interest you most. The purpose of having all this stock market knowledge is not just to make your money grow at a faster clip than simply storing it in a bank account, but also to gain insight in the business world that you might be headed to. There's nothing stopping you from taking your entrepreneurial spirit all the way to adulthood!

QUIZ ZONE

Answers to Chapter 12 - Are You A Smart Investor?

Answer Key...

1. C; 2. B; 3. B; 4. B; 5. A

IF YOU SCORED 5 OUT OF 5

Look out Warren Buffett! You're a true investment genius. Well, let's just say you know a thing or five about investing. You've mastered the basics and can move on to more complicated investment ideas. It might be a good time to talk to your parents or a financial planner to see which types of investments you may not be aware of, but might be interested in learning about.

IF YOU SCORED 3-4 OUT OF 5

Not bad at all. You're on your way to becoming a savvy investor. When you're not sure about what something means with regards to investing your money, it's always best to read up about it and talk to an adult you trust before you plunk your money down.

IF **YOU SCORED LESS THAN 3 OUT OF 5**

You've got some work to do. But at least it's work that will make you richer! Just reading this chapter again will make you a smarter investor. Make it a point to read the business section of your paper every day and follow a stock or two that you're interested in. Also, check out kid-friendly financial websites for extra tips.

CHAPTER 13
Charity and Volunteering: Helping Today Helps Your Future

GIVING and helping others can be a reward in itself. In many cases, you don't even have to give money to help others. Your time is far more valuable to some causes. In return for your generosity you'll be exposed to different people with new ideas. Future employers will also see that you are willing to go the extra mile for what you believe in. It will show that while money is important to you, it's not the only motivation. You have ideals that you will work towards. The strength of your community is important to you, and you will do your best to contribute to its growth.

Fantastic Fundraiser!

ANNIE TACHA, 10, GRAND ISLAND, NEBRASKA

Annie took her love of animals to a different level last year. She started a summer long blitz to raise money for the Hall County Sheriff's Department's K9 unit. The goal? Raise $6,000 to buy a police dog and a bulletproof vest for the working canine. The strategy? Annie, who has a Shetland sheep dog of her own, organized bake sales, car washes, a garage sale, a horse show, and a dog walk to raise the money.

Once word got out through the local newspaper that Annie was raising money to help the Sheriff's Department, donations started pouring in from across the U.S. Chief Deputy Sheriff Chris Rea says Annie's offer to help could not have come at a better time. The Sheriff Department had recently retired one of its two police dogs. And the remaining

There are many ways to give, whether you donate money or time. Setting aside 10% of the profit you make from running your own business is one way. Choose a charity that you care about and make a donation once or twice a year. Research the organization you want to send money to. It's unfortunate, but there are scams out there that exist only to grab your money. Ask your parents if they've ever heard of the group you want to help. Do they have a website? Can you visit their offices? Check if their phone number works (a disconnected phone line is a red flag for a sham organization). Ask for references from other people who have donated or volunteered their time to the group. Ask how donations are used. How much of the money goes to pay for the administration of the group rather than the people it's meant to help.

Sometimes your time is more valuable to those in need than money. Have you ever thought of spending some time at an elderly residence? Many seniors today would not only enjoy your company but would also be interested in learning how to use E-mail to keep in touch with out-of-town grandchildren. Maybe you want to help animals or the homeless in your community. Find out how you can organize a car wash or a walk-a-thon to raise money for causes you care about. Not only will you be helping others, you'll improve your organizational skills in planning the events. Bonus: You get to meet new people and potential clients for your business.

When you're volunteering you also have the opportunity to get the word out about your business. Do you volunteer at the local Y as a soccer coach for younger kids? Let them know what you do to earn a little extra money, whether it's babysitting, mowing lawns, personalized bookmarks, or odd jobs. Don't turn every practice session into an information meeting, but if you simply let them know you also have a job on the side, they or their parents might be interested in hiring you.

dog, an 8-year-old German shepherd named Brix, was later diagnosed with cancer. "We have a lot of budget constraints and we really hadn't planned on needing to buy two dogs," says Rea. "She's not only helping the Sheriff's Department, but all the citizens of this county."

Annie plans to build on this year's successes. Her goal is to keep helping her community. "I'd like to help a different organization in the community each summer," she says. "Next time, I want to do something to help homeless people." No doubt this fearless fundraiser will make good on her promise.

Of course, you shouldn't have strings attached to your volunteering or donations. Helping others is rewarding in itself and a symbol of your character. As relationship columnist Ann Landers once said: "The true measure of a man is how he treats someone who can do him absolutely no good." You will find that donating your time and money can make you happy and proud of your actions!

INTERNET INSIGHTS

www.networkforgood.youthnoise.com:

THIS IS THE WEBSITE FOR THE YOUTH VOLUNTEER NETWORK. CHECK IT OUT FOR IDEAS ON HOW OTHER KIDS ARE HELPING OUT THEIR COMMUNITIES AND WHO'S LOOKING FOR VOLUNTEERS IN YOUR NECK OF THE WOODS.

www.idealist.org:

THIS SITE HAS TONS OF INFORMATION ON ALL KINDS OF VOLUNTEERING OPPORTUNITIES. **CLICK ON THE "KIDS AND TEENS" SECTION TO FIND OUT WHAT YOUR PEERS ARE DOING TO MAKE THEIR COMMUNITIES BETTER.**

www.givespot.com:

SURF THROUGH COUNTLESS IDEAS FOR VOLUNTEERING AND DONATING, EVEN FIND OUT ABOUT CELEBRITY CAUSES. **CLICK ON THE "KIDS AND TEENS" SECTION UNDER THE "RESOURCES" MENU FOR TIPS.**

CONCLUSION
If At First You Don't Succeed...

SO you spent hours, even days, coming up with a great business idea. You even set up shop and tried to drum up business. But your seemingly bright idea is more like a flop than the work of a genius. Your business has just gone bust. Is your life as an entrepreneur over? Did you just blow your one and only chance at running your own business? Of course not – in fact, the opposite is true. You may not believe it right now, but there's a good chance your failure may actually make you a better entrepreneur in the long run.

"I've found that most successful people fail more than once, but they don't give up and that's why they eventually succeed." says Mark Csordos, author of ***Business Lessons for Young Entrepreneurs***. Csordos started his own New Jersey-based mystery shopping business, C&S Mystery Shoppers Inc., when he graduated from college. (Mystery shopping involves hiring people to pose as clients and report back about customer service. Large corporations, like department store chains, restaurants, and banks hire companies who dispatch anonymous shoppers to help evaluate the quality of service their businesses offer.)

When something that you put your heart and soul into doesn't work out, it's okay to feel disappointed and discouraged. The truth is it's no fun to fail. Don't try to deny the fact that you feel miserable and that you need some time to lick your wounds. It might help to talk to someone you trust – a friend, a parent, cousin, aunt or uncle. Express how you feel: You tried so hard and yet still couldn't make it work. Friends and family may not have any magic solutions for you, but just talking about how you feel, and having someone listen to you without judging, can help you work through your hurt feelings. You can even try writing your feelings in a journal.

After a little while you'll be able to see the bigger picture. Chances are there are things you could have done differently to increase your odds of success. Take a look at your original business plan. Analyze the entries of each category: **Mission Statement**, **Market Analysis**, **Promotion**, and **Expenses**. Can you see which area of your business didn't work out? Perhaps your expenses were too high. Or you could have done more market research before jumping into the game.

After analyzing your old business plan, use what you learned to create a new strategy. Advice? If you are convinced that your old idea didn't work out because of something you could improve the second time around, then by all means, try again. But be honest in recognizing the flaws of your old plan. Don't be stubborn. It may be better to scrap your old idea and start over with something new. As well, take the time to bounce your ideas off a friend or parent. Feedback can help shape your ideas further and make them more likely to succeed.

Once you've thought through a few new strategies, *make a timetable for action*. Many people hesitate to try out their new ideas because they are afraid of failing once more. Putting new ideas to the test doesn't guarantee success, but taking the risk to try again builds self esteem and confidence. If you can fail and muster up the courage and strength to try again, you'll feel more self-assured and be open to learning new things along the way.

And you never know, in the process of trying to figure out how to make your business work, you might discover you have other talents. For example, say your cookie business was a flop because you couldn't get your sugar cookies to taste just right. But your cookie decorating skills are tops. You think it's your recipe that stinks, so you try a new one. While the cookies taste a little better, they're still not gourmet. But you still get lots of compliments on your designs. Maybe your artistic flair far outweighs your baking skills. So why not try making personalized stationary or offer your services as a party decorator?

Csordos says it's crucial to keep trying until you find something that works. "If you find something you like, you'll do well eventually," he said. "I've had plenty of ideas that didn't work out. But I kept trying until I *made* it work." The key, Csordos says, is not to take the setback personally. After losing his contract with Pizza Hut, Csordos decided his business idea was still worth pursuing. While it wasn't right for Pizza Hut at the time, he believed that it would work for others. He was right. His persistence and efforts at fine tuning paid off. Csordos eventually netted new clients, including Wendy's, Volvo, supermarket chain ShopRite, and BellSouth, among others. Csordos sold his successful business in

1999 and currently writes, speaks and coaches other young entrepreneurs on how to succeed in business.

So remember, failing every now and then is simply part of life. But that doesn't mean you're a failure. Take it as a challenge. Decide to roll with the punches and press on rather than have them knock you out for life. If you can bounce back and take another crack – or ten – at running your own business, you may find a way to make things work out. "There's just no way around failure," Csordos says. "Sure, you'll get knocked around. But the great thing is that when you're young you can afford to try to start your own business and learn from your mistakes because you have very little to lose and a lot of time to improve."

You might think bouncing back from a setback is easier said than done. That may be true. But it's definitely worth the effort. Consider this: It apparently took Thomas Edison 10,000 experiments to invent the light bulb. Need more proof? Carl Carlson spent 17 years testing and tinkering to make his copy machine – Xerox – a reality. Michael Jordan was cut from his high school basketball team. Good thing he didn't hang up his sneakers for good. And Beethoven's music teacher once told him he was a hopeless composer. Fortunately, he didn't give up on music.

The message is clear: If you think of yourself as a failure, or let others label you a failure, you may be passing up a chance to achieve great things. Learning from your mistakes and risking to try, try again, are the marks of a great entrepreneur.

GLOSSARY

ADVERTISING – creating and posting notices or announcements to create awareness about your business and what it sells.

ALLOWANCE – the portion of money that a parent gives, weekly or monthly, to their children.

BUDGET – an estimate of how much money will be needed to cover all necessary expenses within a certain period of time.

BUSINESS PLAN – a written breakdown of your goals, your ideas on how to achieve them, and the resources you need to make them happen.

CLIENT – a customer who buys a business' products, or pays for their services.

COMMITMENT – a total engagement toward a particular course or venture. Staying power.

CREATIVITY – the ability to use your imagination to think up original and innovative solutions, situations, or products.

CURIOSITY – a desire to discover, know, and learn from the world around you.

DEBT – an amount of money owed.

There are many theories about the origin of the "$" sign. The most popular one is that the symbol started out as the Mexican or Spanish "P's" for pesos. The "$" gradually came to be written over the "P," developing a close equivalent of the "$" mark.

DIVIDENDS – a percentage of a company's profit to be paid out to shareholders.

EMPLOYEE – someone who earns money by working for a person or business.

EMPLOYER – a person or business that pays one or more people to work for them.

ENTREPRENEUR – a person who takes risks in creating an innovative business idea, then moves to organize, manage, and build their company around it.

EXPENSES – money spent in order to start your business and keep it running.

FLEXIBILITY – a readiness to adapt to new, different, or changing requirements.

FOCUS GROUP – a gathering of people to survey. *see market research.

GROSS PROFIT – your total earnings before subtracting the cost of your expenses.

HTML – programming language used to create web pages.

INTEREST – a percentage of money borrowed or invested which you will be charged with, or profit by, respectively.

INVESTMENT – committing your money (into a stock, or account, for example) in order to earn a financial return over time.

LOGO – a name or symbol designed for easy recognition of a business.

MARKETING – strategic planning that is put in place to promote and sell your business' goods or services.

MARKET RESEARCH – data gathered that will help you discover how your job idea will be received by potential clients.

MULTITASK – working on and organizing several projects simultaneously.

NET PROFIT – your total earnings minus the expenses you have incurred in the running of your business.

PROFESSIONALISM – to exhibit a polite, conscientious, and businesslike personality in your work and workplace.

PUBLICITY – having as many people as possible know about the goods and services offered by your business.

RATE OF RETURN – the percentage of money to be profited from an investment or business.

REVENUES – the money that your business generates through the sale of its goods and services.

RISK – the possibility of losing your investment, whether it be time or money.

SHAREHOLDER – *see stock.

START-UP COSTS – the expenses incurred while setting up your business.

The European Central Bank introduced a single currency for Europe in 2002 called the euro. They replace the national coins and bills of 12 participating countries (and three others who may adopt it in the future). Do you know which ones already use the euro? (France, Italy, Germany, Greece, Portugal, Finland, Ireland, The Netherlands, Belgium, Luxembourg, Austria, and Spain) What are the three countries still thinking about it? (Denmark, United Kingdom, and Sweden).

STOCK – a share in, or part of, a business. Once you have bought a stock in a company, you become a shareholder, a part owner in the business.

STOCK MARKET – where the buying and selling of stocks takes place or; the prices of stocks and bonds across the country.

Big money!
The world's largest coins, in size and value, were copper plates used in Alaska around 1850. They were about a meter (3 feet) long and half a meter (about 2 feet) wide. They weighed 40 kilograms (about 90 pounds) and were worth a whopping $2,500.

TAXES – the money people must pay to the government for continued support and public services.

VOLUNTEER – to work for no pay, giving your time and effort in exchange for experience, not money.

Appendix
Jobs in a Nutshell!

NEED some help thinking up great ideas for your business? The following pocket-sized tip sheets will give you a hand in troubleshooting your job idea, or giving it that little twist that will set you apart from everyone else in the market!

BABYSITTING

Basic job description: Taking care of younger kids.

Goods or Service: Service

Seasonal or Year-Round: Year-Round

Give it a twist:
Offer your services even when parents are home. Maybe mom needs you to look after a toddler while she whips up dinner. Expand your service options, too. Help kids with their homework rather than just making sure they stay out of trouble.

A fair price:

Ask around for what other babysitters you know are charging and stay within the same range. If you're the main person responsible for keeping the kid safe, getting him or her ready for bed, and reading a bedtime story, you can charge a little more than, say, if you're just helping mom keep an eye on junior while she bakes some holiday cookies.

Trouble-shooting:

Promising to entertain or tutor kids as well as take care of them is going to keep you plenty busy. Make sure you have a few months experience sharpening your basic skills.

Also, offering activities means you have to take the time to plan ahead. Make sure you have all the props or supplies you need. It's also helpful to know the likes and dislikes of your charge ahead of time.

Spreading the word:

Being a good babysitter requires a lot of organization. Don't forget to make up some emergency contact lists, or some business cards for your clients to pass to friends. For professional looking stationary, check out these creative examples or go to our website at **www.lobsterpress.com**!

GOFER

Basic job description: Making grocery runs at the corner store.

Goods or Service: Service

Seasonal or Year-Round: Year-Round

Give it a twist:
Think of things people forget to do, or simply don't have time to do: drop off parcels at the post office, pick up the dry cleaning, take the garbage to the curb, take the newspaper right up to the door.

A fair price:
You can expect a few dollars for an errand that takes you a couple of blocks from home. Charge a little less if the errands don't involve travel time.

Trouble-shooting:
Safety should always take precedence over getting a job done. Don't try to do more than you can handle. Lugging two bags of groceries is going to take some muscle. It's better to 'fess up than to mess up because a dozen cracked eggs aren't going to get you repeat jobs.

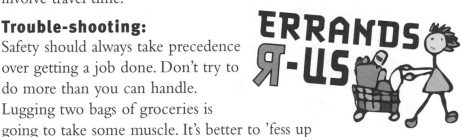

As well, you should never venture to go anywhere that makes you uncomfortable. Learn how to decline job offers politely.

Speedy Scooter
DROP-OFF
& PICK-UP SERVICES

You can always explain your reasons and a good employer should respect them.

Spreading the word:

A successful errand runner must have community contacts. Post your flyers where future clients will be able to see them: your local grocery stores, post offices, and the dry-cleaners. Make your advertising attractive with these creative ideas or look on our website for more inspiration at **www.lobsterpress.com**.

CREATIVE CRAFT-MAKER

Basic job description: Making party favors, decorations, personalized gifts, etc.

Goods or Service: Goods

Seasonal or Year-Round: Year-Round

Give it a twist:
Add service to your goods business. If you are making decorations, why not offer to put them up for an extra fee? Or think beyond things people use. Personalized pet dishes for cats and dogs are sure to be a hit with animal lovers.

A fair price:
Make sure to combine the cost of your materials as well as your time. A couple of dollars for every hour you spend making crafts plus the cost of material should make your products appealing and worth your while.

Trouble-shooting:
If making crafts is what you enjoy most, then that's what you should be spending most of your time doing. Don't pile on the extra services unless it's convenient for you. If it's an extra busy time with school, for example, offer to deliver the party decorations without promising to stick around to arrange them.

Busy-Bee Crafts
& PARTY DECORATIONS

Spreading the word:

Selling your crafts will require some publicity. A professional-looking business card will encourage word of mouth. If you slip a nicely designed business card into each of your packages, it will jog your client's memory on his/her next special occasion. Try creating similar images using the examples in this book to make your cards memorable. Also check out **www.lobsterpress.com**.

DOG WALKER

Basic job description: Walking dogs either in the morning or after school.

Goods or Service: Service

Seasonal or Year-Round: Year-Round

Give it a twist:
There are lots of pets that need your love and care. Bird cages need cleaning, cats need fresh litter boxes, and hamsters need their food dishes replenished when owners are away.

A fair price:
A couple of dollars a day to walk the dog is reasonable. If you need to go to the owner's house to feed the dog, walk it, and do other pet-related chores while they're on vacation, you can charge a little more.

Trouble-shooting:
Caution: There are some exotic pets out there. Although you might love all creatures, great and small, you're probably better off not caring for someone's pet boa. You need to be sure that you know what you're doing.

Also, there's a lot of prep work involved. Be prepared to ask pet owners lots of questions

SIDEWALK SAVVY
DOG WALKING SERVICES

about their pets before they leave you to fend for yourself. Does Spot not like cats? Make sure you know to cross the street if you're headed towards a fine feline while dog walking.

Spreading the word:

Leaving a poster or some business cards at your local pet store is a great way to attract pet owners to your business. Make your advertising attract to pet-lovers with some animal art. Check these examples out, and more at **www.lobsterpress.com**.

DOG-GONE-A-WALKIN'

We acknowledge and respect the licensing agreement that protects the use of certain "clip-art" designs provided by Art Explosion/Nova Development Corporation, and which have been modified for use in this publication. We are in no way suggesting that these designs be reused by the reader. Their use is to enhance the text of this book and to inspire the reader to create such material of their own designing. Any non-authorized use of this clip-art is done with their full knowledge of the consequences.

Trademarks

Band-Aid is a registered trademark of JOHNSON & JOHNSON; **Microsoft Publisher** is a registered trademark of Microsoft Corporation in the United States and/or other countries; **Popsicle** is a trademark of Unilever United States, Inc.; **PlayStation** is a registered trademark of Sony Computer Entertainment, Inc.

Look for these other titles in Lobster Press'
"Millennium Generation Series"
at your local bookseller:

Think for Yourself
A Kid's Guide to Solving Life's
Dilemmas and Other Sticky Problems
by Cynthia MacGregor
ISBN: 1-894222-73-3

Make Things Happen:
The Key to Networking
for Teens
by Lara Zielin
ISBN: 1-894222-43-1

When I Grow Up,
I Want to Be a Writer
by Cynthia MacGregor
ISBN: 1-894222-42-3

7 Secrets
of Highly Successful Kids
by Peter Kuitenbrouwer
ISBN: 1-894222-39-3

www.lobsterpress.com

144